Respect Earned

The Story of Eddie Imada
and the
San Luis Valley Judo Club

Respect Earned

The Story of Eddie Imada
and the
San Luis Valley Judo Club

Published by Matthew H. Dick
Sapporo, Japan
2022

First print edition

Printed by Lulu Publishing

ISBN: 978-0-9910356-3-2

Published by Matthew H. Dick
dickmatthewh@gmail.com

Special discounts are available on quanatity purchases by corporations, associations, educators, and others. For details, contact the publisher at the above email address.

Dedicated to

Edwin Imada

Whitford Myers

Osamu Tahara

Who made the SLV Judo Club possible

Contents

viii

List of illustrations

Acknowledgements

Many thanks to the following people who contributed significantly:

Osamu "Sammy" Tahara shared his family's history.

Eddie's sister Carolyn Imada Lannon responded diligently to my numerous questions by e-mail, providing insights and information on the Imada family and illustrative material related to Eddie's life.

Carl, Michele, and Jeff Myers freely assisted. Carl corresponded at length, filling in various gaps related to SLV Judo and sharing recollections of his father. He also brought the Mizokami court case to my attention. Michele shared memories of SLV Judo and was especially diligent in trying to track down Myers-family photos and newspaper articles. Jeff provided insights into the later years of the club.

Laurier Couture sent photos of the SLV team windbreaker, which I'd entirely forgotten.

Bill Peterson provided useful information on the fate of the club after I left Alamosa.

Toni Bowers sent the 1976 photo of the SLV Judo Club.

Rich Copenhagen provided key information, particularly for the time after I left Alamosa, shared recollections of Eddie (who he lived with for 3 years), and sent illustrative material.

Fred Ogden shed light on changes in judo between the 1960s and now.

My sister, Katherine Dick, lived in Alamosa for nearly 40 years and shared recollections of Eddie, the judo club, and local events. She and my daughter Luella Taranto read and commented on a draft of the book.

Amanda Langdon (Librarian, Adams State University), Amanda Barker (Staff, Colorado Preservation, Inc.), and unnamed staff members for the archives of Denver Buddhist Temple Judo and the Denver Public Library helped with illustration permissions.

Terminology and usage

This book includes Japanese and some Spanish terms. These are defined the first time they are used, but there is also a glossary. In Japanese, nouns lack plural endings, much like the words "moose" and "deer" in English. The context or a numerical modifier defines whether words like this are singular or plural, as in "He saw a moose" versus "He saw several moose." While many writers in English pluralize Japanese words, such as "kimonos" for the plural of "kimono," I avoided this practice and let modifiers or context indicate singular versus plural.

Long Japanese words are composed of two or more roots that are variably hyphenated in English transliteration. For example, the throw "ouchigari" can also be written "ouchi-gari," or "o-uchi-gari," with the three parts in the last rendition translating directly and in order to "major inner reaping." For consistency, I used the transliterations of names of throws and other compound judo terms as they appear in the book Kodokan Judo by Jigoro Kano (2013). Short words (e.g., issei, nisei, kibei) can also be compounds of two or more roots but are generally not hyphenated.

People of Japanese descent living in America are either direct immigrants from Japan and technically still Japanese citizens (and who before and for some time after WWII were barred from becoming US citizens), or US citizens through naturalization or birth. Rather than use the term "Japanese Americans" for any of these, I used "Japanese" throughout simply to refer to people of Japanese descent. Specific clarifying terms in this regard are "issei" (first generation), people who were born in Japan and immigrated to the US; "nisei" (second generation), US-born children of issei and automatically American citizens; and "sansei" (third generation), US-born children of nisei.

I used the masculine pronoun "he" and its derivatives in the strictly grammatical sense to refer to a person of undesignated gender (e.g., It is hard to throw an opponent when he stiff-arms you), disclaiming any sexism in this usage. I tried to avoid the awkward, often hanging plural pronoun "they" in such cases (e.g., It is hard to throw an opponent when they stiff-arm you).

Preface

In August 2021, I tried to locate my high-school friend Kent Myers on the Internet to ask a medical question. I knew he was a physician practicing in Arizona but had lost touch with him for 50 years. Instead of finding him, I found his obituary, informing me he'd passed away in 2000 at age 70— later I learned it was due to a sudden heart attack.

This was a big shock. Three months apart in age, Kent and I were founding members of the San Luis Valley Judo Club in Alamosa, Colorado in 1962 and practiced together for nearly 5 years, a period that profoundly affected both our lives. I realized two things: that the judo club and its inscrutable little instructor, Eddie Imada, were an interesting story, and that if it were to be told, sooner was better than later.

Eddie taught judo to hundreds of kids and young adults in the San Luis Valley across more than 14 years from 1963 to 1977, essentially as a volunteer, and inspired them with his expertise and dedication. Several of his students reached black-belt rank through training at SLV Judo, and two of those went on to reach 6th- and 7th-dan ranks, themselves teaching many students in other parts of the country across five decades.

This is Eddie's living legacy. I know of no plaques or monuments to him in the Valley; he received no formal recognition, no civic awards. I don't know whether he'd have wanted these things, but that's beside the point. He should've had them. If he'd coached a major sport in the school system with the same success he had in raising SLV Judo to regional prominence, he'd have been showered with honors. The main purpose of this book is to tell his story and acknowledge his dedication and service to judo and to the community of the San Luis Valley.

In a broader sense, this book is about judo, Japanese Americans and their history, and life in a small Western town, all of which are, of course, relevant to Eddie's story. I wrote it from my own perspective, which was the only way I could proceed. I was able to locate and contact only a handful of the many people involved in the SLV Judo Club. I could include only what I remembered or could reconstruct from news items, and what contacts remembered and were willing to share.

I've tried to strike a balance between giving readers a sense of what judo is (how the sport is structured; how one learns, trains, and competes in it) on the one hand and boring them to death with technical details on the other. While descriptions are included for several common throwing techniques, interested readers can easily supplement these descriptions with online videos. For example, just now I typed "tai-otoshi" into a Google search and instantly found links to four short videos of this throw. Any of the roughly 68 throws and the various pins, choke holds, and arm bars used in judo can be easily viewed in this way.

Several chapters include some rather esoteric historical content that will be of variable interest to different readers. For example, Chapter 6 (Competition) considers the rules of judo competition and changes to them from the 1960s to the present. Chapter 7 (Intense season) documents the range of judo tournaments available in the Rocky Mountain region in the 1960s. Chapter 8 (The Armory dojo) discusses the development of women's fighting (shiai) competition, which was gaining momentum but not yet officially sanctioned in the 1960s.

I can only suggest you treat this book as you would dinner at a restaurant, where you can shove food you don't like to the edge of the plate and leave it there without offending anyone. In other words, if you get into a part you find doesn't interest you, by all means skim it and move on.

Sapporo, Japan
2022

Chapter 1 – Sammy Tahara

However, in those days, although not sickly, I was, nevertheless, quite feeble. In general scholarly pursuits I was on par with my classmates, but even so I was often treated by them with contempt and despised. From an early age my curiosity had been aroused when I first heard mention of jujutsu, a method of fighting whereby one with little strength, can overcome a physically more powerful adversary. I therefore seriously considered taking up training in this art.

—Jigoro Kano, ca. 1873, in *Judo Memoirs of Jigoro Kano* by Brian N. Watson, Trafford Publishing, 2008

I moved to the town of Alamosa in south-central Colorado the August after 7th grade, at age 12. I was born in Boulder, a mountain town in north-central Colorado, but my family moved to Trinidad, in the southeastern part of the state, when I was three and my father got a job teaching anthropology, sociology, and geology at Trinidad State Junior College, a 2-year institution. After 9 years in Trinidad, he received a job offer from Adams State College in Alamosa and drove the 100 miles there for an interview, with no intention of moving. Unexpectedly, however, after seeing the advantages of the 4-year curriculum at Adams State, where he'd teach only anthropology, he accepted the job.

The move to Alamosa had some drawbacks. Trinidad was a pleasant town nestled along the Purgatoire River in low foothills covered with piñon pines and juniper, at the boundary between the Sangre de Cristo range and the Great Plains. The first time I saw Alamosa was when my parents, sister, and I moved there, and its relative starkness in what appeared to be a largely treeless desert was disconcerting. Furthermore, in Trinidad, we'd lived in a big, two-story, 19th-century brick house in the nicest part of town. In Alamosa, all my parents could find on short notice was a tiny, one-story, crackerbox house built as a speculative rental on 10th Street in the relatively seedy south part of town. It had three bedrooms, each barely big enough for a bed and chest of drawers. The flimsy construction'd been finished just before we moved in, and the newly seeded lawn hadn't yet sprouted in the dry, sandy soil.

I started 8th grade at Evans Junior High School, nearly a mile and a half across town from where I lived, and rather than walking to school as I'd done in Trinidad, I had to get up early to catch a school bus. I soon made friends with some guys who lived within a couple of blocks of me. One was Laurier Couture, who became my closest friend. The others were Ed Reese, who was in my class, and his brother John, older than us by 2 years.

Trinidad was a rough town, with sizeable cliques of Latinos, Anglos, and Italians in the schools. Younger than many of my peers and teased mercilessly due to my surname, I was low in the pecking order and lived in constant fear at school. Nonetheless, I was trying to work things out. I had five "fights" in 7th grade, my last year in Trinidad: a former friend shoving me around at the urging of his newfound gang; three dirt-wrestling matches, two of which I felt I'd won; and one sissy-punching altercation (no blood drawn) in the restroom at a movie theater.

To make matters much worse, my father strictly forbade me any fighting at all. After he caught me in a dirt-wrestling altercation with the kid next door, I got a lecture that lasted a whole dinner hour on the virtues of Gandhian non-violence.

But my father was inexplicably inconsistent. Once, one of his students who was a Golden Gloves boxer visited our home, and my father asked him if he'd be willing to give me boxing lessons. The guy refused. In his experience, he said, teaching kids to box tended to turn them into bullies. The message I took away from this exchange was that I was restricted to non-violence unless I learned to beat the shit out of people, in which case, it appeared, violence would be okay—but I was still prohibited from learning to fight by on-the-job training. This made no sense to me, and from then on, I didn't much heed advice from my father.

By the time I left Trinidad, I was sorely tired of teasing, bullying, and fighting; tired of hiding from small gangs with chains and brass knuckles; tired of the popular sport of pantsing, where gangs took the pants of whomever they caught and left their victims to walk home in underwear.

The only possible advantage I could see in the move to Alamosa was that I was unknown in school and would be left alone. This illusion didn't last long. My first month in town, I spent a lot of time with Ed Reese. One day we were headed home after school on foot and saw a group of 30 or so boys in the open field next to the school. There were cries of "Fight! Fight!" Ed said, "Let's go see what's happening." When we got there, a couple of guys'd just finished settling their differences.

It turned out that, like a turkey arriving for Thanksgiving dinner, we were on the menu. Before I moved to Alamosa, Ed's best friend was a guy named Mike. Now Ed was spending a lot of time with me, and Mike was intensely jealous. As soon as we got to the unruly mob, Mike laid into Ed with his fists. Ed put up a good fight but soon received a deep cut over one eye. With blood running down his face, he was honorably exempted from fighting further.

Mike then laid into me in the same way. Instead of fighting back, I turned my back to him and burst into sobs. I wasn't so much afraid—it happened so fast I didn't have time to be afraid—as just disappointed to the depths of my soul. I'd wanted no more of this sort of thing. I didn't realize then that you never get away from it, in one form or another. Curiously, within a week after the fight, Ed and Mike were bosom buddies again.

From that point on, I was anyone's bitch, relegated to the bottom of the pecking order. My peers felt they could say what they wanted to me without fear of retribution. The day after the fights, a guy named Gary who sat behind me in class said, "I heard what Mike did yesterday. If he ever acts out like that again, I'm going to kick his ass." With this, Gary subtly claimed dominance without lifting a finger.

Later the same year as my humiliation, I myself tried to bully a guy named John Woods, who appeared to be even lower than I in the pecking order. A stout farm boy, he got constant verbal abuse. One day as he was walking to the shops behind the main school building, I made a move on him.

"Hey Woods," I shouted, "where do you think you're going? Come over here, I want to talk to you!" He stopped and stared at me.

"Who do you think you are, talking to me like that?" he said. "If you want to talk, come over here. Otherwise, leave me alone."

John outweighed me by 20 pounds, and fighting him would've been like fighting a threshing machine. I just walked away, and that was that— except for the profound shame I feel to this day, that to bolster my ego I tried to inflict on someone else the same thing I was enduring.

4

What I finally realized was that John Woods had self-respect and let hateful speech slide off him like sweat on a hot day. Furthermore, I'd landed in a social structure where my peers'd established boundaries among themselves from kindergarten through 7th grade. People verbally abused John, but I never saw anyone try to fight him. That'd been settled long before. In contrast, I was unknown and had to be tested, and I'd come up short.

This was my social status in the fall of 1962, when my classmate Kent Myers informed me a Japanese college student was soon going to offer judo lessons at the high school and asked whether I'd like to participate. I had no idea what judo entailed, but I said yes. I was mildly surprised when my parents—to whom I'd mentioned nothing about my trials at school over the past several years—readily assented.

⌐

Those of us who showed up for the first judo lesson in October 1962 were in 6th to 11th grade, aged roughly 11 to 16. The others I remember for sure were Kent Myers, Carl Myers, Laurier Couture, and Harold Hock. We utilized the wrestling room on the ground floor of Alamosa High School, a two-story building of tan-colored brick built in 1921 and past its prime. **[Illustration, p. 146]** Curiously from the standpoint of traffic safety, it fronted on Main Street toward the west end of Alamosa's business district, though admittedly there wasn't all that much traffic.

The wrestling room was a grungy 20 by 30 feet, the floor covered with thick, old, padded mats surfaced with blue plasticized canvas. Wrestling season hadn't yet started; the room'd aired out over the summer and wasn't yet unpleasant. Along the west wall, opposite the entrance from the hallway, intermittent, multi-paned banks of windows extended from waist high to the ceiling, facing out onto lawn and side street. Spaced along the wall lower than and between the windows were old, cast-iron heating radiators. At night, the high-ceilinged room was well lit with fluorescent lights.

For sport apparel, we'd been told to bring sweat pants or shorts, and a heavy-duty, full-sleeved sweatshirt. Some of us showed up in a sweatshirt and jeans; others had a full sweat suit. We milled around savoring faint eau de wrestler for about 10 minutes, until Whitford Myers—municipal judge, organizer of the judo lessons, and father of Kent and Carl—arrived with our instructor, a short, gaunt Japanese guy who couldn't have weighed more than 120 pounds fully clothed and soaking wet.

"Hi," said the Japanese guy, "my name is Osamu Tahara, but everyone calls me Sammy. I am from Yokohama, Japan." With bangs of straight, black hair hanging into his eyes and thick, black-frame glasses dominating a narrow face, Sammy seemed to have a lot of suppressed kinetic energy to him; he was always in a hurry and seemed to be in motion even when he was sitting still. **[Illustration, p. 148]**

Sammy'd already changed to his old, worn judo gi, or uniform, which was grayish rather than white, with a tattered black obi, or belt, around his waist. His judo rank was shodan (1st dan; 1st-degree black belt), earned in Tokyo. The first thing he did was line us up in a row in the seiza kneeling position—trunk erect, shins under thighs, one foot over the other in the rear, hands on thighs. He took the same position facing us.

"When we start class and when we finish, we bow to each other. We are not praying to any gods; it is only to show mutual respect. I will say 'kiotsukete,' which means 'attention,' and then 'rei,' which means 'bow.'" He demonstrated how to bow, bending forward, placing hands to the mat and forehead near it, and then back. Upon his call, we all came to attention and bowed, we to him and he to us.

"Okay," said Sammy, all of us remaining in the seiza position. "First, I want to tell you is what judo is. It means 'gentle way.' It is a sport for physical fitness and for mental and moral discipline. It is no good if you want to learn it for street fighting. They do street fighting in the bars downtown, and if you try to use judo against those guys, even if you are good at it, you will get hurt. But the main thing is, street fighting is degrading. You use judo only as a last resort, if it can help you defend yourself. That is the moral part of judo."

This was a disappointment. I'd been thinking about payback at school—but at least deterrence might still be in play.

"Judo," Sammy continued, "was founded in 1882 when Jigoro Kano started the Kodokan in Tokyo. The Kodokan is sort of a Mecca for judo. People who practice judo are called 'judoka.' You are now judoka. Before Kano came along, people in Japan practiced jujutsu, which included striking techniques and many other dangerous moves designed to hurt or kill someone. Kano removed the harmful techniques and kept the safe ones for practice as a sport."

Finally Sammy said, "Do you have any questions?"

"Yes," one of us said. "You said judo is also a mental discipline, but what's the mental part?"

"Outwitting your opponent is part of it," Sammy said. "The other part is that sometimes judo hurts so much, you want to quit, but you don't."

When we met him, Sammy Tahara was an economics student in his senior year at Adams State College. At 28, he was old for a college student. Though he must've been born around 1934, I never asked how he'd fared during WWII in Japan. His father'd been drafted as an infantryman into the Imperial Army and fought in the Philippines, where he was captured and finished out the war in an American POW camp. This was not a bad experience; Japanese soldiers who survived the act of being captured were treated well. The senior Tahara was a skilled baseball player and earned respect in games between the Japanese prisoners and their American guards. He viewed his POW experience as one of the best times of his life—plenty of food and rest, daily baseball, camaraderie, no one shooting at you—the closest thing to a real vacation he'd ever had.

The Tahara family were butchers and, post-war, erected a three-story building in the Kanagawa ward of Yokohama. The building had a butcher shop and outlet store on the ground floor and living quarters for the extended family on the upper two floors. With his father's encouragement, Sammy studied English and graduated in economics from a university in Tokyo. Although he'd been groomed as a financial manager for the family business, Sammy chafed at this simplistic role and convinced his father to support a further 4-year education in the US, arguing that he could become fluent in English, familiar with Western economic practices, and better prepared for the arena of international finance when he returned to Japan. His father, perhaps thinking back on his own positive experience with Americans, went for it.

After I got to know Sammy, I asked how he'd ended up at Adams State. "Oh, that's simple," he said. "When I was looking for a school to attend, not knowing which ones were good and which were bad, I just chose the first one on the list."

How Sammy came to teach judo in Alamosa was almost equally haphazard. The story Carl Myers remembered was that Sammy ended up in municipal court in front of Judge Myers, having been accused of stealing a loaf of bread from a local store. The Judge asked Sammy about his circumstances, which Sammy replied were bad. He'd run out of money, didn't have enough to eat, and was having trouble finding part-time work to support himself. Learning that Sammy had a black belt in judo, the

Judge ruled he'd dismiss the charge if Sammy agreed to offer judo lessons, by which he could earn some money.

There's some uncertainty about the details of this story. Carl wrote, "I cannot absolutely swear that Sammy lifted a loaf of bread. That does seem incredible, hungry or not! Perhaps it was some other kind of misunderstanding? Somehow, though, he was brought into municipal court."

Fate works in convoluted ways, but this was extreme. Due to baseball in a POW camp in 1945, alphabetical selection of a university, and an alleged stolen loaf of bread, we ended up with a judo teacher in Alamosa in 1962.

⌒

"Okay," said Sammy, after starting the class, "the first thing we do is exercises, both to loosen up and to build strength so we don't get hurt. So please stand up and spread out."

Facing us, he led us in exercises—various stretches standing and sitting; standard pushups and sit ups; judo pushups (legs widely spread, body moving down and returning in a circular motion, using a greater range of muscles than regular pushups); supine leg raises; duck walking; and exercises to build strength for mat work.

The mat-work exercises were grueling and I came to hate them. One was to lie prone and inch yourself across the mat by extending your forearms and pulling your body forward using only your biceps and shoulders. Due to the friction of clothing against the mat, this took a lot of effort, but we did it several times back and forth the length of the room. Another was a similar thing on your back, moving the length of the mat by twisting your body side to side like a landed fish trying to return to the water, without using arms or legs. There were two ways to do this, forward and backward, and they were both exhausting.

When we finished the exercises, Sammy said, "Now that you are warmed up, I will teach you how to fall. If you don't know how, chances are good you will get hurt. When you do know, it is very rare to get hurt, no matter how hard you land. In judo, we call falling techniques 'ukemi.'"

Falling in judo is quite safe if you do three things. The first is to master the breakfall, which is to slap the mat hard with your free arm and open palm as you land. The energy of this downward blow reduces the force with which your torso hits—your arm literally breaks your fall. This also requires you to turn toward your side, so that you don't land flat on your back. Second, always keep your chin tucked to your chest, to avoid landing on your head or suffering whiplash. Third, always keep your legs apart and straight so they hit the mat separately. When you get thrown, your legs are the farthest-out and fastest-moving part of your body, and you can injure a knee or foot if one leg lands on the other.

Sammy first taught us backward and side breakfalls, beginning with the supine position, then the sitting, crouched, and standing positions. Next he taught us the forward breakfall, where you land in the prone position, breaking your fall with your forearms and palms slapping the mat. We practiced this from the kneeling and standing positions. The forward breakfall is jarring and unpleasant, but necessary in certain situations, as when you twist out of a throw and land face first on the mat.

The most advanced ukemi technique is the forward roll, practiced on both the right and left sides, where you do a quasi-somersault, rolling along one curved arm and landing with some force in a side breakfall with the other. The purpose of the forward roll is to simulate, by yourself, the act of getting thrown. Forward rolls are difficult and painful at first; your elbows get in the way, and you soon learn why you need to tuck your chin and keep your legs apart.

We finished the lesson practicing forward rolls. At the end, Sammy lined us up in seiza position and we bowed out.

"Another thing," he said. "You make a standing bow whenever you come onto the mat or leave it. Also, you bow when you enter the workout room and when you leave it. Always. This is just to show respect for the place you practice, which we call 'dojo'—even this ugly wrestling room is a dojo, ha, ha." He showed us how to do a standing bow.

"Okay, see you next lesson, same time," Sammy said before he bowed off the mat, bowed out of the dojo, and disappeared to the locker room to change back into his street clothes.

That was our first judo lesson. It was exotic and interesting enough that we wanted to return for lesson two. Little did we know some of us would attend hundreds of the same over the next 5 years.

I don't remember how many times a week we practiced under Sammy or what we paid. I'll defer to Carl Myers, who remembers sessions of "a couple of hours" twice a week and a fee of $10 a month, most or all of which would've gone to Sammy.

Chapter 2 – The Valley

Blanca scene of threats to Japanese—*Capt. Joseph C. Monnig of the courtesy patrol said today that he and other officers had been in Blanca* [a town in the San Luis Valley, Colorado] *Wednesday night for the second time to investigate rumors of a planned uprising against Japanese in the area. Monnig reported he had about thirty citizens of Japanese descent in the Blanca area. Most of them are respected citizens. Monnig attributed the rumors to young hoodlums who think less then they talk.*

—*Alamosa Daily Courier*, 11 December 1941

In 2002, 40 years after the beginning of the story I'm telling here, I was living in Taos, NM. A friend and his wife drove down for a visit from Boulder. Having gotten a late start, they decided to overnight at a motel in Alamosa before continuing the 90 miles on to Taos the next day. My friend's spontaneous remark about Alamosa was, "God, what a pit!"

I jokingly replied, "Hey, watch it, man, that's my hometown you're talking about." In fact, I was a little miffed. The longest I lived continuously in Alamosa was only 5 years, but they were formative years in which I made the transition from childhood to quasi-adulthood. It is more my hometown than anywhere else I lived.

I can understand why my friend viewed Alamosa as a pit, for I'd had somewhat the same reaction when I moved there. Coming from the east, Highway 160 traversed 25 flat miles of alkaline soil and scrub brush before it took a jog (magnanimously called Broadway) across the Rio Grande River to become Main Street. East Alamosa, the last, mile-long stretch before the highway reached Main, was a strip-burb of mostly old, sketchily maintained homes on large lots with typical Western landscaping—

sometimes a small patch of lawn but mostly tumbleweeds, greasewood brush, derelict cars, old farm equipment, small corrals, and barns.

The approaches from the other cardinal directions were similar but even more abrupt in their transitions from sticks to town. Alamosa greeted travelers arriving from the south on Highway 285 with a large, triangular lot filled with used farm equipment.

Alamosa (Spanish for cottonwood grove) has always been a work in progress. It started with a bang in 1882 as an extension of the Denver and Rio Grande (D&RG) Railroad. One day there were only tents for railroad workers; the next day, when the tracks heading straight as a ruler west-northwest from Fort Garland reached the Rio Grande, prefabbed buildings were brought in on flatcars. The town sprouted up almost overnight. By the 1960s, its population was 6500.

Laid out in a grid of streets nestled along the southern bank of the Rio Grande, the bulk of Alamosa comprised roughly 13 blocks north to south and 20 blocks east to west. **[Illustration, p. 144]** To the west, the town ended with the grounds of Adams State College and associated housing. The two main, perpendicular thoroughfares were Main Street (east–west) and State Street (north–south). Wide enough for four lanes of traffic, Main Street was densely packed on both sides with one- and two-story commercial buildings, some of them dating to the late 1800s. **[Illustration, p. 145]** State Street, crossing Main toward the east side of town, turned abruptly rural to the north as it traversed the river on its way to the municipal golf course, and to the south as it passed 13th Street on its way to the cemetery, regional airport, and rodeo grounds.

Alamosa started as a railroad town and remained one. Cutting right through the middle of town like an axe wound, parallel to and a block south of Main, was the cindery track complex of the D&RG Railroad, an extensive staging and switching facility a block and a half across. At the edge of town to the east were a roundhouse, train-repair shops, and big fuel tanks.

The nicest part of town was North Alamosa, extending the six blocks north of Main Street, with relatively old, shaded neighborhoods and well-kept lawns, culminating in the Adams State campus to the west. South of the tracks, the town was seedier, especially on the west side, where people didn't pay as much attention to their lawn or didn't have one.

The Alamosa Chamber of Commerce might wince at this physical description of its town, which is not essentially different now than it was in the 1960s. I can take the edge off by noting that travelers just passing through, regardless of direction, see only the least attractive parts of town. Furthermore, a town is not only streets and buildings but also people, set in a broader landscape both historical and ecological. Many people who move to Alamosa dislike it at first, grudgingly come to like it, and finally love it. The town motto could be, "It might be a pit, but it's *our* pit."

∽

Alamosa lies a little north of the center of the San Luis Valley, or "Valley," as it's called locally, a large intermontane basin mostly in south-central Colorado but overlapping into New Mexico. If you travel to the Valley expecting to find a river canyon flanked by wooded slopes, you'll be disappointed. The Valley floor is 55 miles at its widest east to west and 105 miles north to south, roughly 3500 square miles in area, nearly half again the size of Delaware. While it's not truly flat—elevations range from 7000 to 8000 feet, with an average of 7700 feet—when you see it from any of the flanking mountaintops, it appears breathtakingly vast and flat, like a child of the Great Plains banished to the middle of the Rocky Mountains.

The Valley is spindle-shaped, demarcated by the San Juan Mountains to the west and the Sangre de Cristo Mountains to the east, which converge at Poncha Pass, the northern limit. The San Juans are a lower, broader range, and from the center of the Valley, you can't tell whether they're merely foothills or are going to prove to be more formidable once you get into them (they do).

On the other hand, there's no doubt about the Sangres being mountains. Mt. Blanca, a little north of due east from Alamosa, rises 7000 feet above the valley floor to reach 14,347 feet and is capped with snow from late fall until early summer (hence the name blanca, Spanish for white). **[Illustration, p. 143]** Mt. Blanca doesn't look very impressive from Alamosa because it's over 20 miles away, but it's not much lower in elevation than California's Mt. Whitney, the highest mountain in the continental US at 14,494 feet. Gathered around Mt. Blanca are four other peaks above 14,000 feet. Thirty miles to the northwest is another massif of sharp 14,000 footers, collectively referred to locally as the Crestone Needles, that look like canines in the maw of an enraged dog.

Another thing you might expect of a valley is that it is verdant, but again, looking across the expanse of the Valley from a surrounding mountaintop, its overall effect is light brownish or yellowish or gray green, like a desert—which it is. The average annual precipitation in Alamosa is only 7.3 inches. Much of the valley floor is sandy, sparsely vegetated with grasses and low desert shrubs—greasewood (locally called chico), rabbitbrush, and the occasional sage.

As if to affirm the Valley's identity as a desert, predominantly southwesterly winds for the past few tens of thousands of years have deposited Sahara-like sand dunes along the edge of the Sangres in a crescent roughly 8 miles long by 4 miles wide. Lying between Mt. Blanca and the Crestone Needles, these aptly named Great Sand Dunes are the tallest in North America, some reaching 750 feet. You can easily see them from Alamosa 25 miles away, both due to their height and because they're higher in elevation.

It takes some fortitude to live in the Valley. If you have even a hint of agoraphobia, you won't like it there. The sky is huge, visible from horizon to horizon any way you turn, like you are at sea. The sun shines roughly 280 days a year. Trees occur mostly along rivers, or were planted for shade in the towns and as windbreaks around isolated farms. Vast areas are treeless, which makes visitors from wooded parts of the US nervous, as though there'd be nothing to hold them down when the wind blew.

"How can you stand to live in such barren country?" my mother's cousin from Vermont once asked on a trip though Alamosa. My mother replied, "Well, last time I visited Vermont, I couldn't see a damn thing because of all the trees."

Summers are bearable, with the hottest days typically in the 80s F and rarely exceeding 90 F. The winters can be brutally cold, not infrequently dipping into minus digits Fahrenheit at night and occasionally reaching to -40 F. There are rarely more than a few inches of snow on the ground. Not much falls, and the little that does gradually sublimates in the dry air. Some winters, weeks go by with the temperature not rising above freezing, and the whole valley glistens with snow and hoarfrost in the high, pure air.

All right, the Valley doesn't sound too bad, not unbearable, but there are a few more things to mention. In March and April every year, a cold wind blows virtually nonstop, carrying with it a fine silt that invades your home through poorly sealed windows and doors, and sometimes seems to get past even well-sealed ones. It's relentless—a desert version of the Chinese water torture. Furthermore, if you're anywhere near standing or flowing water in summer, you're besieged by hordes of persistent mosquitos. Finally, there's the elevation. It takes a week or two to acclimate when you arrive from sea level. Once you're acclimated, the elevation's not a problem unless you have a bad heart or chronic breathing problems. Another effect is that the thin air filters out a lot less UV light than air at sea level, and fair-skinned people burn fast.

There's a lot of green in the Valley, but it's most obvious up close, near water—and water is rather abundant for a desert. The main aquatic feature is the Rio Grande, which enters the Valley from the northwest at South Fork and flows east-southeast to Alamosa, shortly after which it turns sharply south and continues into New Mexico on its way to the Gulf of Mexico. Several smaller rivers and creeks flow into the Valley, those in the north tending to disappear into the dry soil, those in the south converging with the Rio Grande.

Two underground aquifers comprise the other main source of water. One lies close to the surface and is easily tapped for pumping wells. In a low area in the northern part of the Valley, this upper aquifer reaches the surface, giving rise to marshes and the permanent San Luis Lakes. In places where subsurface water comes close to the surface and evaporates, it draws alkali salts from the soil and deposits them in a crisp white crust that incongruously looks like snow.

The other, deeper aquifer is artesian. Confined under pressure between layers of clay, it gives rise to scattered natural, permanent springs, and when tapped by wells hundreds to thousands of feet deep, flows to the surface continually without pumping.

This abundance of water in a climatological desert has consequences both aesthetic and economic. The contrast between zones of lush, verdant vegetation and stark, brownish desert is striking—a photographer's paradise. You see this effect along rivers, around natural and artificial ponds, and around farmland. When you trudge across miles of dull brushwood and sand to come suddenly upon an oasis of sedges and horsetails around the standing pipe of an old but still-functioning artesian well, it's like finding an emerald in the rough.

Standing marshes and seasonal river marshes attract migratory waterfowl in great abundance. Roughly 20,000 sandhill cranes fly into the Valley in fall and depart in spring, filling the air with their haunting, rusty-hinge calls. Hundreds of thousands of ducks and geese migrate through seasonally, warming the soul with the sights and sounds of their passing and lining the pocketbooks of local economies, for the Valley attracts waterfowl hunters from across the US.

From the strict economic standpoint, irrigation via canals large and small, diverted from rivers or fed by thousands of wells, allows the cultivation of farmland—by the 1960s, 590,000 acres (about 925 square miles) of it, or roughly 25% of the Valley's area. In the last three decades of the 1800s, the Valley became a breadbasket for Colorado and beyond. It supplied wheat, hay, and potatoes early on, with an increasing diversity of crops in the 1900s—barley, sugar beets, spinach, lettuce, carrots. The total population of livestock—sheep, cattle, horses, pigs—has historically outnumbered that of humans, which in the early 1960s was 40,000.

Needless to say, the main industries of the Valley and its predominantly rural inhabitants are farming and ranching, or support for these activities. If you want to buy farm equipment, Alamosa is a good bet. If you want a Mercedes Benz, you'd better go to Denver.

$\backsim$

The Valley has a fascinating history. Suffice it to say that it has, in whole or in part, belonged successively to nomadic Native Americans, Spain, the Republic of Mexico, the Republic of Texas, the US Territory of New Mexico, the Territory of Colorado, and finally (since 1879) Colorado State.

In 1849, Hispanic settlers from northern New Mexico—former Mexican citizens, mestizos, and Native American in-laws—established the first permanent settlement in the far-southern part of the Valley. Named Plaza de los Manzanares, the town lay near the present-day village of Garcia on the New Mexico border. They founded another town in 1850 near San Luis. These and subsequent Hispanic settlements in the southernmost part of the Valley have Spanish names—Mesita, Antonito, Conejos, Romeo, San Acacio, San Luis, La Jara—and the mother tongue of many of the inhabitants to this day remains Spanish.

The 1860s saw an influx of settlers to the Valley, prominent among which were Army veterans—many of them from northern Europe—who'd served the Union cause and could apply the scrip they received upon termination of service toward the purchase of homestead land. While settlements in the southern part of the Valley remained largely Hispanic in culture and Catholic in religion, settlers in the northern part tended to be Anglos, that is, people of northern European descent and typically Protestant. In 1872, for example, a couple hundred German immigrants started a cooperative community west of Del Norte but soon split up as independent farmers. In the 1870s, the region around Monte Vista saw an influx of Swedes, Englishmen, and Midwesterners.

Significant numbers of Mormons began to arrive in the 1870s. A group of around 70 settled on land purchased from Hispanic owners in the southern part of the Valley in 1878 and founded the town of Manassa in 1879. Within a decade, the Mormons established the communities of

Ephraim, Richfield, Morgan, and Sanford, with a sizeable contingent around La Jara. Though subject to discrimination for their religion, the Mormons were tenacious, hardworking, and self-sufficient and earned the grudging respect of their neighbors.

⌒

One other group of settlers deserves special mention, given that they sprang from the culture that invented judo—the Japanese. The first Japanese immigrants arrived in the Valley as transient railroad workers in the late 1800s and early 1900s and decided to stay. According to the US census, 11 Japanese were living in Conejos County in 1910.

Japanese began entering the Valley in greater numbers in the 1920s as the result of events on the West Coast. There were already many Japanese immigrants in California—by 1920, roughly 50,000 issei ("first generation," immigrants from Japan) and 20,000 nisei ("second generation," American-born children of issei) inhabited the state. Starting as contract laborers when they first arrived in America, the issei excelled at agriculture; by 1920, they owned 75,000 acres of California farmland and rented, sharecropped, or leased another 383,000 acres. As they went along, they improved land no one else wanted, pioneered the California rice industry, and developed the truck farming of vegetables to a high science.

At the same time, anti-Asian racism in the US, and especially in California, resulted in a series of increasingly restrictive laws to prevent the entry of Japanese to the country and limit their activities once they'd arrived. The US Naturalization Act of 1870 limited American citizenship to "white persons and persons of African descent," thus barring immigrant Japanese from citizenship, although the Constitution guaranteed citizenship to their children.

In a direct reaction to the Japanese success in agriculture and "yellow-peril" jingoism, California passed the Alien Land Law of 1913, which prohibited non-US citizens from owning agricultural land. To circumvent this law, issei Japanese began to buy land in the names of their American-born children or to transfer titles to their children and establish themselves as trustees. The California Alien Land Law of 1920 largely closed these loopholes.

While all this was going on in California, real-estate companies in the San Luis Valley were buying cheap desert land, developing it as irrigated farmland, and selling it to farmers. Starting in 1909, the Costilla Estate Development Company built reservoirs for irrigation in the area south and west of San Luis, laid out several new towns on the sites of old Hispanic settlements, and went into business. Japanese began to settle in this area, especially around San Acacio.

In the early 1920s, Valley land companies, aware of the problems Japanese farmers were facing in California, contacted Japanese Associations there to advertise that fertile farmland was available. It was a strong selling point that Colorado had no alien land laws like those in California. California's loss was Colorado's gain. A scant 600 acres of vegetables were under cultivation in the Valley in 1923; by 1925, Japanese-owned farms alone had 4000 acres under cultivation. Census records show that by 1930, at least 233 Japanese—mostly skilled farmers and their families—had settled in the six counties of the Valley. Japanese continued to arrive through the 1930s, and by 1937 the Alamosa-La Jara Japanese Association had a large enough membership that it built a Buddhist church in downtown La Jara.

A last pulse of Japanese immigrants came to the Valley shortly after the onset of war with Japan in December 1941. In February 1942, President Roosevelt issued his notorious and ill-advised Executive Order 9066, which directed the establishment of military areas "from which any or all persons may be excluded," allegedly for protection against espionage and sabotage. Area 1 comprised the entire western flank of the US from Washington State to southern Arizona, and the main group to be excluded was the Japanese, non-citizens and citizens alike.

Japanese who were already outside Area 1 could stay where they were. For about a month, West-Coast Japanese had the option to voluntarily relocate outside the military exclusion zone—at their own expense—and some people who had friends or relatives in the San Luis Valley relocated there. After this option closed, the roughly 120,000 Japanese left in Area 1 were non-voluntarily relocated to internment camps scattered around the western US.

⌒

Having just read a CliffsNotes-like treatment of Alamosa and the San Luis Valley, you might reasonably ask, "What does any of this have to do with the preceding chapter about a judo lesson?" In one sense, nothing at all. You can practice judo anywhere, regardless of the local environment or history. But to understand how unlikely a place the San Luis Valley was for a thriving judo club, you should understand what a basically harsh place it is, populated in large measure by hard-bitten farmers and ranchers.

Alamosa in the 1960s was a Merle Haggard, Okie from Muskogee sort of town, where "Leather boots [were] still in style for manly footwear; beads and Roman sandals [wouldn't] be seen." The most popular spectator sports were football and rodeo. Judo uniforms, Japanese words, and bowing fell in the same category as beads and Roman sandals—or so one would've thought.

Chapter 3 – Some people

Uki-waza – Floating Throw. Having broken your opponent's balance to his right front corner, you block his right foot with your left foot and throw him over you by falling on your left side. For the technique to be successful, excellent coordination is necessary when sacrificing your standing posture to make full use of the power available.

—*Kodokan Judo* by Jigoro Kano

We had our second judo lesson. Sammy bowed us in and led us in stretching and strength exercises, including the miserable mat-work training. We practiced the full suite of ukemi breakfalls and forward rolls. Sammy watched with a sharp eye for sloppiness. Keep your chin tucked! Legs apart! Place your non-slapping hand on your waist!

This became the warm-up routine for every practice session as long as our judo group continued. Once we'd learned to fall, it wasn't really necessary to practice ukemi every session. Frequently there were new students, however, and they needed to practice it, so we all did it. Necessary or not, it was good physical training.

After about a month, when we finally became proficient at forward rolls on both the right and left sides, Sammy had someone kneel and we dived over him, ending in a forward roll. As time went on, we did forward rolls over two or three people kneeling side by side. Then we went over a belt held horizontally three feet off the mat. Finally, we were having contests to see who could dive over the most people or highest belt, ending in a forward roll.

After we finished our second-lesson warm-up, Sammy taught us our first throw. "I'm going to show you one of the simplest throws, called uki-waza," he said. "In English, this means 'floating technique,' but we always use the Japanese names. That way, if you go to a country where they don't speak English—like Japan—they'll know what you're talking about."

Sammy showed us how to grip an opponent, taking a handful of sweatshirt at the elbow and another handful at the opposite lapel. Your opponent grips the same way, elbow and lapel. You can grip right or left handed, but in the beginning we only gripped right handed—right hand on the opponent's lapel, left hand on his sleeve. In judo, the thrower is called "tori" and the faller "uke" (from the same root as "ukemi").

Uki-waza is simple—tori uses his leg to blocks uke's and falls to his side, using his backward momentum to toss uke overhead. It's easy to learn and provides excellent falling practice, because uke essentially ends up in a forward roll as he goes down.

After demonstrating the technique, Sammy had us pair up. It's easiest to throw your opponent if he's moving in the direction you want to throw him, so we moved backward and forward in pairs, taking turns throwing one another. It almost goes without saying that when one practices throws in this manner, it's without any resistance at all from uke. In fact, uke's more or less compliant, graciously going exactly the way tori wants him to go. One can "learn" throws in this manner, but a different level of learning or proficiency is required if uke resists to any extent.

Many of the throws classified as hip and hand techniques require that tori pivot into uke so that he's facing the same way as the latter. An example is o-goshi, the major hip throw. This is the technique most commonly seen in action movies, where the hero pivots in, puts his arm around the villain's waist, and throws him forward over the hip.

In addition to walking back and forth to practice this sort of throw, we learned a method called uchikomi, meaning "driving in," in the sense of driving in a nail, also referred to as "doing fits" or "fitting." In uchikomi, uke stands still and tori repeatedly pivots in, gets his hip into position, and lifts uke slightly off the ground but doesn't complete the throw. Tori typically does nine repetitions and then throws on the tenth.

By now you're scratching your head and thinking, man this could get boring in a hurry. Is this idiot going to spend the next however-many pages describing lesson by tedious lesson, and throw by tedious throw? The answer is no.

With lessons one and two, I've basically described the following 7 months of judo practices. At the start of each class, we warmed up and did ukemi. We learned roughly one new technique each week, practiced that one, and reviewed and practiced ones we'd already learned. I refer to techniques rather than throws, because judo also involves pinning techniques (osaekomi-waza), and Sammy taught us some of these as we went along. There are choking and arm-bar techniques as well, but these are generally not taught to beginners.

By the following May, we'd learned perhaps 25 techniques, give or take. After we'd learned a few throws and pins, we began to do randori, or free practice, where two partners spar using any techniques they can but without maximum resistance. This also became part of our routine.

↜

Throwing techniques (nage-waza) in judo are classified in two ways, one functional and the other pedagogical. Functionally, the first subdivision is between standing throws (tachi-waza) and sacrifice throws (sutemi-waza). Standing throws, where tori remains standing, comprise hand techniques (te-waza), hip techniques (koshi-waza), and leg techniques (ashi-waza). Sacrifice throws, where tori himself uses a controlled fall to throw his opponent, comprise supine (ma-sutemi-waza) and side (yoko-sutemi-waza) techniques. Uki-waza, the first throw we learned, is a side sacrifice technique.

Pedagogically, a set of 40 basic throws, standardized in 1895 by Jigoro Kano at the Kodokan, is divided into five groups of eight throws each, with the groups increasing in presumed level of difficulty from the first to the fifth. This classification is called the Go Kyo No Waza (Five Groups of Instruction). The Kodokan recommends these groups be learned in order, although this is rarely followed. As a case in point, uki-waza, the first throw Sammy taught us, is in the fifth and supposedly most difficult group. Actually, roughly 68 throws are used in judo, but the 40 throws in the Go Kyo No Waza form the basic core of instruction.

There's a practical problem in following the Go Kyo order. When beginners join an ongoing class and have learned to fall, and unless the classes are divided into beginning and advanced students, the beginners will start with whatever throw the instructor's teaching at the time. Even if the instructor initially adheres to the Go Kyo order, some students will learn the throws out of order.

↩

As the winter progressed, our class gradually increased in size. The high-school wrestling season began in November, with daily afternoon practices, and our evening dojo, rather than having a faint eau de wrestler about it, now stank of rancid sweat and unwashed jock straps. Furthermore, with the onset of cold weather, the radiators along the outer wall fired up, and we could get burned as well as bruised when we accidentally fell into one of them.

After about a month, when it looked like the class had some staying power, Judge Myers brought an order form for judo gi from a supplier in Denver, and we all ordered uniforms. As soon as they arrived, Sammy showed us how to wrap and tie the belt (which was white, for beginners) over the uniform top—starting with the middle of the belt in front of the waist, looping the ends around the back to the front again, tucking one end under the other layers in front, and tying a square knot, so that the ends project horizontally rather than vertically. He also showed us how to fold the uniform into a compact carrying bundle and to tie the bundle properly with the belt, as though it were around the waist of a little bundle-person. All of this validated our expectations for learning an ancient martial art, and we followed Sammy's instructions meticulously.

By the end of the school year in May 1963 (I was now 13), our judo group had 20 or more members and we loosely referred to it as "the judo club." We had judo uniforms. Falling was by this time instinctual. We knew enough techniques to make randori interesting, yet were learning new things every session.

We were well on our way along the path of judo, but for one big problem. Sammy Tahara was due to graduate from Adams State in May and would leave soon thereafter for a job in New York. We thus had to find a new instructor, or we were finished.

↩

I didn't know Sammy well when he taught us judo, although I reconnected with him years later. I had only a glimpse into his life outside our classes. One day, through some coincidence, we were on the way to practice together, and he had to stop by his residence for something—maybe his judo gi. He inhabited a basement room in an old, two-story wooden house occupied entirely by male college students. The whole place was cluttered and grungy, as one might expect for a bunch of guys who no longer had their mothers around to browbeat them.

As we were about to leave the basement, one of the other students shouted from the first floor, "Hey Tahara, you slant-eyed little prick—while you're down there, put my wash in the drier!"

This didn't seem to faze Sammy, who shouted back at him, "Sorry, can't do it, I have to go," and we left.

I was shocked and outraged. "Is that how those guys treat you? It's horrible. I'm going to tell Judge Myers—he'll straighten them out."

"No, it's okay," Sammy said. "That's how we talk to each other. Usually I call him 'shit-for-brains Polack' and some other things, but I don't have time right now. We don't want to be late for class."

Much later, Sammy told me his years in Alamosa were the best time of his life.

⌐

Our organizer, Judge Myers, was a big-boned man, about 6 feet tall, a little on the heavy side when I knew him, with a longish, rounded face and respectably short, sandy hair. **[Illustration, p. 147]** He typically dressed well in a suit and tie or less formally in dress pants and a white, button-down shirt. He had a deep voice, which was an advantage in his profession. Although he could project a certain personal gravity as the occasion demanded, he had a good sense of humor and smiled often. If I had to describe him with one word, it'd be unpretentious. He was approachable and put people at ease. When we built or moved a dojo, he showed up in old jeans and a T-shirt and worked with the rest of us, joking as we went along. I liked him a lot.

Whitford "Whit" Whited Myers was born on 8 August 1920 in Raton, New Mexico, roughly 90 miles southeast of Alamosa on the other side of the Sangre de Cristo range. His father worked for the post office. His mother, an elementary school teacher, was the daughter of Greeley W. Whitford, who at one point was a district judge in Denver and later became chief justice of the Colorado Supreme Court. After high school, Whit entered the University of New Mexico in Albuquerque. Times were tough, and he worked at any part-time job he could find at the going wage of 25 cents an hour to put himself through school—janitor, waiter, and in one instance, pressing presidential candidate Wendell Willkie's suit.

While at UNM, Whit enrolled in a government-sponsored flight-training program at Cutter-Carr Flying Service in Albuquerque. During a night-flying lesson in August 1941, he was at the controls when he noticed that part of the landing gear was broken and dangling loose. The pilot, Bill Cutter, took over, dropped distress flares (apparently they had no radio), and circled the city until he'd used up most of the fuel, in case of a crash. The ground crew at the airport west of the city flagged down passing motorists to light the runway with their headlights, and Cutter successfully landed the plane on one wheel.

Whit joined the US Navy Air Corps in February 1942 and trained at Long Beach, California and Corpus Christi, Texas. After flight training, he served as a pilot in scouting and utility squadrons in the region of the Panama Canal and Cuba. In July 1944, he married Helen Comstock of Santa Fe, New Mexico, a fellow student at UNM who'd also learned to fly at Cutter-Carr. Whit was discharged from the Navy in October 1945.

After the war, Whit and Helen moved to Denver, where they both finished their BA degrees and completed law school at the University of Denver. Helen was admitted to the Colorado Bar in September 1947 and Whit in March 1949.

They moved to Alamosa in 1949, where Whit first practiced law with Merle M. Marshall, a prominent local attorney. After two years, he opened his own practice or perhaps took over Marshall's. In 1958, he became an associate municipal judge, which he did part-time in addition to his law practice. On 1 October 1965, he was sworn in as a judge for the Colorado 12th Judicial District, which comprises the six counties of the San Luis Valley, whereupon his wife took his place as municipal judge. Whit and Helen had four children from 1949 to 1958—in order, Kent, Carl, Michele, and Jeff—all of whom participated in judo. **[Illustration, p. 155]**

According to Carl Myers, both his parents were progressive jurists. The Miranda warning became required practice in police arrests after 1966, but even before that, Whit and Helen routinely advised people in police custody of their legal rights and strongly urged them to seek an attorney before questioning.

I asked Carl why his parents'd moved to the San Luis Valley. He wrote, "I remember asking Dad that very question when I discovered that in Denver, lawyers made a lot of money. He said, 'Yes, some do, but they don't get to live here!'" Both Whit and Helen'd grown up in small Western towns, and the Valley was their kind of country.

According to Carl, Whit Myers's passion aside from the judo club was fly-fishing on the upper Rio Grande. He spent long winter evenings in a corner of the basement, tying his own intricate flies to mimic insects in various stages of development. After his involvement with the judo club wound down, he leased a cabin at Wright's Ranch above Creede and adjusted his court calendar to suit his fly-fishing schedule.

↩

Among the original group that started under Sammy Tahara, Laurier Couture, Kent Myers, and Harold Hock soon became my closest friends in Alamosa. Laurier, Kent, and I were roughly the same age whereas Harold was 3 years older, a high-school senior when we were freshmen. Carl Myers, another charter member and Kent's younger brother by 2 years, was in a different grade in school, and we didn't associate outside judo.

Harold Hock lived in north Alamosa with his mom, Lorraine, who worked as a secretary for the electric company. I don't know what happened to his father, but Harold had an uncle in La Jara. According to Harold, the uncle was physically abusive, which led Harold to teach himself karate for defense. Maybe this was why he started judo as well.

In his high-school yearbook photo the year I met him, Harold looks adult and distinguished, like a junior diplomat in an overseas embassy. His high-school footprint was much like my own. The same yearbook shows he belonged to the Science Club, Quill and Scroll journalism club, and National Honor Society in his senior year, but that was it, no sports, no student government, nothing that demanded much of his time. He had other things to do with his time.

Harold's passion was military history, especially European. He read about it. He studied French and German so he could understand relevant terminology and pronounce names. What he did with most of his spare time was play military board games. The most general of these was *Stratego*, but he favored Avalon Hill games, including *Stalingrad*, *Bismarck*, *D-Day*, and *Waterloo*. These latter games allow opponents to replay actual battles on realistic maps, using historically accurate allocations of military forces and taking into account such factors as terrain, weather, supplies, reinforcements, and chance.

I know about this because Harold needed opponents and co-opted Laurier, Kent, and me, among others, into this role. We became his war-game groupies. We spent a lot of winter weekends at Harold's place playing against him or one another. He'd studied the actual battles and held forth on strategy as he invariably defeated us, cackling about how militarily foolish we were. He knew the various generals' names on both sides and lectured on what they did during the actual battle, and what they should've done. When things got tense on the battlefield, he'd break out into karate moves against us, stopping short of actually hitting. This was irritating.

He also claimed to be an orchestra conductor and often lectured us on the proper hand motions used in conducting. I think this was total bullshit, just his seeing how much dissembling he could get away with.

Having learned somewhere about Crêpes Suzette, perhaps in French class, Harold decided we were going to make them one weekend. He behaved as though he was a master of the recipe and had prepared it many times before. He assigned each us to bring an ingredient—flour, milk, butter, eggs—but since we were too young to purchase alcohol (he was too, for that matter), he provided the alcoholic ingredients. Recipes typically call for Grand Marnier, orange Curaçao, or triple sec, but Harold apparently read "and" for "or" and used all three. Or maybe he just wanted as much alcohol as possible. In any case, after endless commentary on the proper preparation and flaming of crêpes, we all sat down to gorge ourselves.

Looking back, I realize we were starstruck at hanging out with a senior when we were freshmen. Harold could be overzealous, but he was fun to be around.

⌒

Laurier Couture (who we all called "Larry") lived with his parents and two sisters in a pre-WWII wooden house a block from where I lived. He received his unusual given name from his father, Roger Lafayette Couture, a Franco American from Maine who'd married a local girl and ended up in the Valley after WWII.

Laurier was my best friend from 8th grade through high school, not only because we lived near one another but also because we had similar ideas on the best means of frittering away time in a small town. He was about my height, five-ten, a little lighter in build but physically tough. His high-school photos show shortish black hair and the no-nonsense facial expression of a member of the French Resistance.

Laurier and I had various adventures and misadventures in high school. The November of our freshman year, we went duck hunting. People typically leased or owned ponds and constructed blinds from which to hunt, or hunted along irrigation ditches with farmers' permission. The closest place we could reach on foot was a complex of three large sewage-disposal ponds half a mile east of our neighborhood. These were surrounded by an 8-foot-high chain-link fence designed specifically to keep people like us out.

We both had 16-gauge shotguns borrowed from our fathers, with or without their knowledge. When we reached the ponds and were standing there discussing where to hunt, Laurier's shotgun suddenly discharged, blowing a crater in the semi-frozen ground to one side of us. In our post-accident reconstruction, neither of us could figure out quite how it'd happened, but it was a monument to the adage, "never point a gun at anyone you don't want to shoot."

Still shaky from our gun-safety lesson, we climbed the embankment to the closest pond. There, distant but within shooting range, was a single, bobbing duck. Casting sportsmanship to the wind, we both shot at it through the chain-link fence, and one or both of us hit it.

It was de rigueur that you always retrieve your quarry, no matter what, but this was an unusual case, as we had no retrieving dog. It was a gray, blustery day; the ground vegetation was brown and the trees bare of leaves. After considerable discussion, we climbed the fence, doffed our clothing, and swam out through the choppy water to the duck—both of us, because we both had to prove we could do it and wanted instant backup in case one of us got hypothermia.

We retrieved the duck. I forget who took it home, but considering its source, I doubt anyone ate it.

Another example of extracurricular activities was our sling phase—not the Y-shaped slingshot with a heavy rubber band, but the Biblical type. Laurier was the first to make a sling, after seeing a David-and-Goliath movie on TV. We fabricated and tested slings until we had an acceptable model with nylon bootlaces for the cords and a leather patch for the pouch. We found adequate stones along the shoulders of roads to use as projectiles but eventually carved molds in scraps of lumber and cast tetrahedonal projectiles from lead.

We routed our walks home from school through the wide track complex of the D&RG running through town so we could practice. Our goals were accuracy, maximum damage, and maximum distance. Accuracy was just something that came from practice. For maximum damage, we hurled large stones against the refinery-scale fuel tanks near the railroad shops. We succeeded in putting dents in what must've been at least 3/8-inch steel, and whoever dismantled the tanks must've wondered how the dents got there. For a distance test, we got increasingly far away—up to three blocks—from Boyd School in our neighborhood. The classrooms on each floor had multi-paned banks of windows 10 feet high, and we could hear the breakage of windows to gauge whether we were making the distance with our lead projectiles. This was a shitty thing to do, but we did it anyway.

⤶

Kent Myers was a high-end achiever, gifted both academically and athletically and already strong from sports. His freshman year, he played football, wrestled, and pole-vaulted. His sophomore year, the wrestling team won the league championship and Kent "lettered" in wrestling. He was thus eligible to wear a school letter jacket, which he was inseparable from thereafter. The difference in our freshman photos in the high-school yearbook is striking. While I'm mouselike (and my photos only grow worse in subsequent years), Kent looks remarkably like Ken of Ken-and-Barbie fame, fully mature, chiseled and handsome.

As I remember it, Kent did so well in junior-varsity football his freshman year that the coaches identified him as a future star quarterback. To their great disappointment, he didn't continue with football, giving the reason that it interfered with judo. This drew lasting enmity towards the judo club from the football coaches, who were powerful in the high-school staff hierarchy and may've thrown a wrench in our further use of school facilities. But that was okay, for around that time we moved to our own dojo.

Kent participated in the high-school orchestra; at one time or another belonged to the Science Club, Photography Club, and Math Study Group, as did most of us; and in his senior year was president of the National Honor Society. During his junior and senior years, however, he quit organized high-school sports, except perhaps for pole-vaulting, and focused his considerable athletic ability on judo.

Kent was among the Harold-Hock groupies during our freshman year but otherwise moved in different circles than Laurier and me. He would've disdained swimming in sewage-disposal ponds and breaking school windows. Looking back, I realize I don't know what Kent did with his time outside the judo club and school, though when we finally got into judo competition on a regular basis, there wasn't much spare time.

One activity Kent, Laurier, and I did participate in was what might be called "sandlot hockey," when the City flooded part of Cole Park in winter to make an outdoor skating rink. The rink wasn't used much, because the ice was rough and the temperature usually too cold for pleasure skating. I don't remember how the tradition got started, but on Saturdays, a haphazard assortment of 10 or so high-school boys would converge on the rink. Most of us had figure skates rather than hockey skates, and we used whatever we could find for sticks (brooms, broomsticks, tree branches) and a puck (tin can, rock, rubber ball). We played for hours in the bitter cold, with a fire alongside the rink for intermittent warmth.

Kent and his best friend Steve McGuinn showed up the rest of us by jumping, on their skates, a 3-foot-high wall of railroad ties stacked toward one end of the rink. No one else even attempted it. They gained notoriety one weekend by skating for miles up the Rio Grande. The ice was probably solid enough in the cold, but the very thought of breaking through intimidated the rest of us.

Kent was a giver of nicknames. For example, he assigned "Mort" to me, "Coot" (for Couture) to Laurier, "Chicken Hawk" (for Hock) to Harold, and "Chief" to a Navajo college student who was briefly in the judo club. Not everyone received a Kent-nickname; indeed, the recipients seemed to be a small subset of his acquaintances. No one else used these names, and I found mine to be vaguely irksome.

School studies came easy to Kent. Whereas I usually took home an armload of books for homework, I rarely saw him with books outside school. In addition, he seemed to have a more active mind than the rest of us. One topic he rambled on endlessly about was the possibility of a SCUBA device that removed oxygen from the surrounding water, eliminating the need for an air tank. He claimed he had it all worked out but stopped short of building a prototype.

As another example, after our sophomore year, he and I took a summer course in German together so we could fit in a full two years in high school. He read up on means of learning in one's sleep and rigged up a tape recorder on a timer to play German vocabulary during the point of the sleep cycle best suited for subconscious learning. Maybe it worked—I did as well as he in the German course, but through conscious, brute-force memorization.

Chapter 4 – Eddie Imada

Groceryman Hero—*Sergeant Fred Nishitsuji, a front-line nisei soldier, was interviewed recently in a narrow slit-trench on the Buna front by Don Caswell of the United Press, while Japanese bombers roared overhead. Among the things Sergeant Nishitsuji told the U.P. reporter was that his girl's name is Mary Kunugi of Los Angeles, who evacuated to Blanca, Colo. After the war the nisei sergeant said that he was going to open a grocery store in Los Angeles. . . New York's newspaper PM headlined the U.P. story on Nishitsuji: "Don't Shoot Fred—He's No Jap Jap."*

—*Pacific Citizen*, Thursday, December 31, 1942

With Sammy Tahara gone, we waited until we got word that judo practices would resume. When we reconvened in the wrestling room, Judge Myers showed up with a short Japanese man who he introduced as Mr. Edwin Imada. Five feet, three inches tall, Mr. Imada was clean-shaven, with a full head of medium-length, jet-black hair. More muscular and filled out than Sammy, he was 38 years old. **[Illustration, p. 149]** The Judge explained that the Denver School of Judo had sent him to Alamosa to be our instructor. Furthermore, Mr. Imada'd just started a job as a seasonal groundskeeper at Adams State and taken up residence in a small house directly across Main Street from the high school.

We were astounded. Here we were, a raggle-taggle band learning judo in a borrowed wrestling room at the ass end of Colorado, yet someone thought enough of us to send an instructor from the Capital City. It wasn't as though Mr. Imada was just taking a bus across town, either; he'd uprooted his whole life to come to us. That established a debt of gratitude we'd have to work hard to pay.

While I forget exactly when our new instructor arrived, I believe it was in June 1963, not long after Sammy departed. This makes sense, because summer was when he'd be most needed in his new job as groundskeeper.

The Judge went on to explain that in judo and other Japanese endeavors, the teacher is called "sensei" (teacher), a title applied in the same way a coach might be called "Coach Smith," although after the surname. We hadn't called Sammy "Tahara Sensei" because he preferred to be called Sammy. This lapse in etiquette notwithstanding, the Judge made it clear we were to address our new teacher as "Imada Sensei." We used this at first but soon shortened it to just "Sensei." His friends, family, and work colleagues called him "Eddie," which I'll use here.

I don't know the train of events that led the Denver School of Judo to send us an instructor, but I can make some educated guesses. Judge Myers probably started the process in motion before Sammy Tahara left Alamosa. He undoubtedly knew Sammy'd be graduating and departing in May. By this time, it seemed clear that the judo club was viable and would continue if we could find another instructor. But where to find an instructor?

Denver had a large, vibrant Japanese community, and the Denver School of Judo, founded in 1953, was the largest and most influential dojo in the Southwest. On 11 March 1962—roughly 7 months before we had our first judo lesson in Alamosa—the Denver School moved into a large, warehouse-like automotive garage that'd been renovated into a dojo to the cost of $100,000 (equivalent to $923,000 in 2021), located at 2020 Arapahoe Street in downtown Denver. **[Illustration, p. 159]** The head instructor was Tooru Takamatsu, ranked 5th dan but soon to become 6th dan. **[Illustrations, pp. 152, 156, 158, 161].**

The Judge may just have gotten Takamatsu Sensei on the phone and said, "Hello, my name is Whitford Myers. We have a judo club going here in Alamosa and our instructor is leaving. I'm wondering whether you could send us another one."

I doubt this approach would've gotten very far. Takamatsu Sensei'd be scratching his head, wondering who the hell Whitford Myers was and how much of a judo club they had out there in the sticks, anyway. When Judge Myers was shopping around for a new judo instructor in 1963, he needed someone who could introduce him at the Denver School—he needed credibility—and this may've come through his law practice, where he got to know and respect the Japanese farmers in the Valley, and vice versa.

In 1962, Whit Myers took on a high-profile case as attorney for Mizokami Brothers Produce in the Valley town of Blanca. Mizokami was the largest grower of summer spinach in the US and shipped most of its product, which was widely recognized as being of superior quality, by railroad to the East Coast for processing. In August 1962, FDA inspectors took samples from 10 railroad carloads of Mizokami spinach and claimed to have detected, by paper chromatography, the prohibited pesticide heptachlor in two of them. This resulted in an embargo on the spinach. Mizokami lost what it'd shipped East and had to disc under 335 acres of prime spinach that year, suffered a reduction in prices for its product the following year, and lost some of its best East Coast customers.

Mizokami denied having ever applied heptachlor, and subsequent analyses by the FDA using more-reliable gas chromatography found no heptachlor in the shipments in question. The FDA admitted that its initial analyses had been in error (oops!), and Mizokami then sued the US government to recover $543,880 in consequent losses. The US Court of Claims eventually resolved the case in Mizokami's favor in 1969, awarding $301,975 in compensable damages. That was a lot of money in an era when Whit Myers received $15 an hour for legal services.

Harry Sumida, another prominent farmer in Blanca and one of the Japanese leaders in the Valley, may've been the Judge's intermediary with the Denver School. He was the outgoing president of the Valley chapter of the JACL (Japanese American Citizens League) in January 1963 and had many connections in Denver. His two young sons, Harry Jr. and Randy, joined the judo club at some point, and once or twice a week their father drove them to practices in Alamosa—a 60-mile round trip. Mr. Sumida had background in judo himself, because later when we were training for competition, he personally coached his sons.

↬

By whatever channel the Judge contacted the Denver School, they took him seriously and wanted to help, but who to send? It had to be someone of black-belt rank willing to uproot himself and his family, if he had one, to a small town on short notice for an undetermined period of time.

Wait a minute, what about Eddie Imada? Eddie is single, self-employed as a custom gardener, has no relatives left in Denver, and was just promoted to shodan. [Illustration, p. 152] And, frankly, he's recently been a pain in the ass—didn't someone complain he came to practice drunk a couple times? Let's ask him.

The last bit is not just my speculation. Later I met many of the young judoka at the Denver School and became friends with some of them. I asked one of them why Eddie'd been willing to move to Alamosa, where he'd miss not only his friends, but also the whole Denver scene—Japanese restaurants and festivals and small theaters showing samurai flicks, which he loved. My friend said that it hadn't entirely been Eddie's choice; that he'd occasionally shown up for evening practice if not drunk, at least after having a beer or two—something the Denver School wouldn't be happy with.

Whether or not this was true, I got to know Eddie well enough later to doubt he'd have volunteered spontaneously to move to a cow town like Alamosa—he might've had some help in volunteering. I can imagine Takamatsu Sensei calling him into the glass-fronted office looking out onto the broad expanse of tatami matting at the Denver School for a conversation that went something like this:

TAKAMATSU: "Good to see you Eddie. Congratulations again on your promotion to shodan. How're you doing?"

IMADA: "Thanks. Things are going okay; I have a lot of work lined up this year. What's up?"

TAKAMATSU: "Recently a judge in Alamosa in the southern part of the state contacted me. They have a new judo club that's been active for about half a year. They're all fired up, but their instructor is leaving and they need another one."

IMADA: "That's too bad. I hope they find one."

TAKAMATSU: "This is what I wanted to talk to you about. I'm wondering whether you'd be willing to move down there for a while to help them out."

IMADA, pausing, shaking his head: "*Me*? Why me? No, I don't want to do that. I'm happy here, and I've got my gardening business."

TAKAMATSU: "The guy I talked to in Alamosa said he has a full-time job lined up for you as a groundskeeper at the local college, and a free place to stay. You'd be doing the same kind of work you're doing here.

IMADA: "But I don't know anyone there. Besides, a little nipponjin [Japanese person] like me wouldn't fit in very well in a town full of rednecks."

TAKAMATSU: "The truth is, Eddie, you're not fitting in very well here right now, either. I heard you came to practice drunk a couple times."

IMADA: "*What*? I never came to practice drunk. I might've had a beer or two after work, 2 hours before practice, but I was okay by the time I got here."

TAKAMATSU: "If someone thought you were drunk, it was as bad as being drunk."

IMADA: Silence.

TAKAMATSU: "Eddie, you're one of the best guys I've got. You're a great teacher, and young people like you. But now, when you're not at judo or at work, you're pissing away your time partying. You're better than that. You need some direction, some responsibility. This is a good chance for you. Not many guys get a shot like this to have their own dojo."

IMADA: Silence.

TAKAMATSU: "Eddie, I really want to help those guys in Alamosa. The JACL is behind them, and it'd look good for the Denver School. I'd consider it a personal favor if you'd agree to go down there, at least for a year. If you don't like it, you can always come back. But who knows, maybe you'll like it."

IMADA, after a long pause: "Okay, Sensei, I understand what you're saying. Can I have some time to think it over?"

TAKAMATSU: "Yeah, please think it over. I appreciate it. But give me an answer one way or the other as soon as possible."

I really don't know what actually transpired. It might be that Takamatsu Sensei put out the word and Eddie did simply volunteer, attracted to the idea of a steady job with regular hours and some benefits, without the hassle of running his own business. Maybe he was just jaded with Denver. In any case, he went.

Eddie would receive no compensation to teach judo in Alamosa, except that the judo club would cover his house rent of $35 a month. Takamatsu, however, was not expecting Eddie to do anything he himself wasn't doing. No one at the Denver School got paid for teaching judo. The money that came in from fees, benefit events, and community donations was barely enough to cover the large dojo's renovation loan and utilities. The higher-ranking sensei like Tooru Takamatsu, George Kuramoto, and Fred Okimoto showed up for classes several times a week, as did the many lower-ranking black belts who came to train but also helped teach. There were various classes for women, kids, beginners, and advanced students that met at different times or ran concurrently but separately on different sections of the dojo's big mat. Everyone, instructors and students alike, paid a $15 initiation fee when they joined the dojo and a monthly "tuition fee"—in late 1963, $10 a month for men and boys, $7 for women and girls, $5 for black belts, and $4 for additional members from the same family.

The Denver School also had a board of officers—president, several vice-presidents, secretaries, treasurers, auditors, and a lawyer—all of whom were volunteers.

So what is this thing, judo, such that Eddie was willing to uproot himself to a town of strangers for at least a year and to donate his weekday evenings? Judo is a gift from your teachers. You benefit from their teaching physically, mentally, and morally. You repay them with respect and by becoming a better person than you would've been without them. You also pay the debt forward by teaching others.

∽

The story of Eddie's family typifies those of many Japanese in America in the first half of the 20th century. It is a story of dogged perseverance in the face of suffocating, larcenous racism, which makes it all the more incredible that Eddie would uproot himself to a small town where he knew no one to teach a group of mostly non-Japanese students. Of course, we knew nothing of Eddie's history when he arrived.

Eddie Imada was born in Sacramento, California on 1 June 1925 and given the name "Jun." Jun is a common male name in Japan, but in Eddie's case it might've also reflected a play on words with the English "June," the month of his birth. To an English speaker, Jun sounds like June. This must've occasioned a lot of teasing in school, for Eddie eventually begged his father to give him an English name. By the time he was 14, his name'd been legally changed to Edwin Jun Imada.

Eddie's grandparents, Wakazu and Kizie Imada, immigrated to the US in 1908 with Eddie's father, Ichiji, who was 3 years old. Ichiji's only sibling, his sister Fusako, was born in Sacramento in 1910. The 1920 US Census listed Wakazu's occupation as "farmer" and his employer as "fruit farm."

Ichiji later changed his name to Tom Ichiji Imada, and everyone called him Tom, so I'll use that name here. **[Illustration, p. 150]** In 1924, at age 19, he applied for and received a US passport. To do so, he filed a notarized document in which a lawyer in Sacramento attested, "I have known the above-named Ichiji Imada personally for 4 years and know him to be a native citizen of the United States; and the facts stated in his affidavit are true to the best of my knowledge and belief."

Later the same year, Tom used the passport to travel to Japan to marry Fujiko Nakashima, an 18-year-old woman from Kumamoto province—Eddie's mother. This was an arranged marriage, a process called "omiai," mediated through a matchmaker in the US or Japan.

While omiai was traditional in Japan, arranged marriages in the US were likely due more to legal and demographic constraints. Legally, California anti-miscegenation laws at the time prohibited marriages between Caucasians and Japanese. Demographically, in the 1920s the ratio in California of adult Japanese men to women of childbearing age was two or three to one. These constraints meant that many men of Japanese descent wanting to build a family in America had little choice but to seek a wife in Japan.

The marriage license, issued by the American Consular Service in Kobe, listed both Tom and his bride as residents of Kobe. Tom clearly didn't reside in Kobe, nor likely did his bride, so the Kobe residences may've been merely a consular formality for the issuance of a marriage license. Tom spent over 6 months in Japan, returning to the US in January 1925, separately from his new wife.

Fujiko arrived in the US by May 1925, because Eddie was born on June 1 that year. She bore two daughters in close succession after Eddie, but the marriage didn't last. The story Eddie told is that his mother ran away with a Filipino worker from the farm where Tom was employed, taking her daughters with her. By 1930, she was no longer with the Imada family, and at some point she and her daughters returned to Japan, leaving Tom and Eddie in America with Tom's parents. After his mother's departure, Eddie was likely cared for by his grandmother Kizie, who didn't speak English.

Tom's American-born sister Fusako moved to Japan for a period of nearly 5 years from February 1924 to December 1928 (aged 14–18). This wasn't an uncommon practice; the term "kibei" applies to nisei sent from the US back to the mother country to be educated in Japanese language and culture. Interestingly, 1924 was the same year Tom traveled to Japan to marry.

In 1929, a year after she returned to the US, Fusako married a Japanese immigrant 8 years her senior named Yamato Hara, who'd been in the US nearly a decade. I mention these details about Tom's sister because she and Eddie remained close throughout their adult lives. Eddie's sister Carolyn wrote about her, "My aunt spoke perfect English, as did my dad. I think she worked at Bullock's Department Store in downtown Los Angeles. She always had a very dignified and elegant way about her."

By 1935, Tom Imada'd moved to Los Angeles, and in 1938 he remarried, through another arranged marriage, to a woman 11 years younger than he named Hatsuye Toyoda. Hatsuye was another kibei; born in Los

Angeles in 1916, her family'd sent her at age 8 to relatives in Otago village near Kumamoto, Japan. She returned to the US in her mid-teens, speaking little or no English, and reunited with her father in Stanton, now part of greater Los Angeles, before marrying Tom.

Hatsuye and Tom's first child, Evelyn, was born in Los Angeles in 1939. The 1940 census lists Tom and Eddie (age 14) still there, working as custom gardeners. Tom's second marriage was successful and stable, and Hatsuye bore another seven children: Jane (1940), Alvin (1943; died early in childhood), Leonard (1947), Carolyn (1948), Beverly (1950), Ronald (1953), and Stanley (1954). While these were all technically Eddie's half-siblings, none of them referred to him as anything but their brother.

Hatsuye never did become entirely fluent in English. According to Carolyn, "she spoke a type of 'pidgin' English, though she could always say 'goddamn it' very clearly. She managed to communicate with her employers [as a housekeeper] and was able to make purchases without any problems."

Hatsuye may've sometimes used her lack of fluency to advantage. Once a local market was giving away a free drinking glass with each purchase, and she walked out of the store with a whole case of six glasses, to the horror of whichever family member was with her. If she'd gotten busted, Hatsuye could claim she'd misunderstood the sign about the free glasses—which maybe she had.

The Imada family was in Los Angeles in December 1941, when the US declared war on Japan. As the result of President Roosevelt's Executive Order 9066 of February 1942, mentioned in Chapter 2, the Imada family— Tom, Hatsuye, Eddie, Evelyn, and Jane—was first relocated to a temporary assembly center near Yuba City, about 40 miles north of Sacramento. They had to leave behind everything except what they could carry in the way of personal effects, bedding, and clothing. In September 1942, they were transported to the euphemistically named Granada Relocation Center, also called Camp Amache, on the dry, bleak plains of southeastern Colorado. Eddie was 17. **[Illustration, p. 151]**

Eddie's grandmother Kizie'd left the family sometime after the death of her husband in 1936 and ended up in the even hotter, bleaker Poston internment camp near the Colorado River in southeastern Arizona, where she died in 1943. Tom's sister Fusako Hara and her family were also in the Poston camp, so Kizie may not've died alone.

Like many former internees, Eddie never said much about Camp Amache. When I asked him about it once, his only comment was, "There were teenage gangs, and it was rough." He told his friend Rich Copenhagen that he'd been quite the ladies' man in the camp, involved with both young women around his age and, in some cases, women their mothers' age.

⤶

Much has been documented and written about Amache and the other internment camps. By October 1942, Amache housed 7567 internees and had become the 10th largest town in Colorado—it had 2000 more people than Alamosa at the time. The Camp proper was 160 acres in extent and consisted of 29 blocks of barracks arranged in orderly rows and columns, each block containing 12 residential barracks; a recreational barrack; an H-shaped building with communal toilet, bathing, and laundry facilities; and a mess hall.

In addition to the barracks blocks, there were municipal buildings such as a hospital, fire department, post office, motor pool, several churches, a cooperative store, police department, newspaper, and schools. In the erection of Camp Amache, 569 structures were built in all, including 348 residential barracks. The whole shebang was surrounded by a barbed-wire fence, a jeep-patrol road, and eight guard towers with searchlights, initially manned in shifts by 134 armed military police. This armed presence was relaxed later on, when it became clear the internees weren't bent on rebellion or escape.

The barracks were lightly constructed and without insulation, though Granada is one of the hottest towns in Colorado in summer, and temperatures in winter frequently reach below freezing and occasionally below 0 F. Each residential barrack was divided by single-layer sheetrock partitions into six single-room "apartments." The apartments came in three sizes, allocated according to family size. As a family of five, the Imadas had the largest size, 25 by 20 feet, or 500 square feet. Single adults and married couples without children got smaller rooms, often sharing them with strangers.

The rooms had a brick floor and were provided with a coal-burning, potbellied stove; a canvas cot with a thin mattress and two woolen blankets for each person; and a single-bulb overhead light. When the internees arrived, there was no shelving or other furniture. They soon remedied this as well as they could with scavenged lumber and eventually erected privacy partitions with sheetrock or cloth dividers. They could mail-order such things as linoleum, cloth, or small electrical appliances, or buy them from the cooperative store, but the initial accommodations must've been a stark shock for people who'd just left their own comfortable homes.

Camp internees came from all walks of life, and the Relocation Authority employed those of working age in jobs, where possible, consistent with their pre-camp experience as doctors, teachers, nurses, firemen, cooks, farmers, policemen, reporters, mechanics, farmers, laborers, and so forth. I use the term "employed" loosely here, as the internees received only a pittance compared to wages on the outside: doctors and dentists received $19 a month and unskilled workers $8 to $12 a month. To put this into context, the Federal minimum wage in 1942 was 30 cents an hour, or about $50 a month. Possibly the only reason the internees got paid at all was that the Relocation Authority wanted to avoid subsequent charges of using slave labor.

The entire Granada Relocation Project encompassed 10,423 acres, of which Camp Amache was only the residential part. Most of the working internees were employed in agriculture on the Project acreage, growing a wide variety of vegetables as well as feed crops for the chickens, pigs, and cattle they raised. The idea was that the camp would produce enough to feed itself, which it soon did. As experienced farmers and gardeners, Tom and Eddie Imada almost certainly worked on the camp farm.

Former internees later recounted that the worst thing about the camp, other than the stinging injustice of being there in the first place, was the lack of privacy. They could hear their neighbors through the thin walls separating adjacent rooms. They had to line up for sinks and toilets in the morning, laundry facilities, showers in the evening, and each of the three daily meals in the mess halls. The women's toilets lacked stall doors, nor were the shower heads separated by enclosures—also true of the men's facilities, but it didn't bother the men as much. The seating in the mess halls consisted long rows of picnic tables with attached benches, and families lost their cohesion as kids and teenagers tended to sit with one another rather than with their parents.

Even during the war, it was possible for internees to apply to relocate outside the camp. Some young people resumed interrupted college educations or found jobs on surrounding farms or ranches; other people with particular skills found jobs elsewhere in the country—as long as they stayed out of the West Coast exclusion zone. In all, 953 mostly young men but also a few women escaped Amache by joining or being drafted into the US armed services. Among the men, 31 were killed in action and 105 wounded.

I don't know when or where Eddie started judo, but it's possible he started in Camp Amache, for the opportunity was there. Rather than mope around bemoaning their fates, the internees organized a wide variety of educational, artistic, and athletic activities, including sports teams. An article from the *Granada Pioneer*, the Camp Amache newspaper, on 14 November 1942 (less than 6 weeks after Eddie arrived) announced that more than 50 students were practicing judo under instructors Sakichi Takao and Takaharu Kawashima, in 2-hour sessions held 4 days a week. The dojo was located in the recreation barrack in Block 8E, next to Block 8F where the Imadas lived. George Kuramoto, one of the founders of the Denver School of Judo in 1953, was also interned at Amache. He left the camp in 1944 and would've overlapped almost exactly with Eddie.

Eddie registered for military service in August 1943 at age 18, as required by law, listing his employer's name and address as "War Relocation Authority, Amache, Colorado." He enlisted in the US Army in September 1944 at age 19 and reported for duty at Fort Logan near Denver.

No one remembers much about his Army service. Eddie told his sister Carolyn that after basic training, he'd been scheduled for deployment overseas as a replacement with the famed 442nd Regimental Combat Team (a unit composed entirely of nisei Japanese that fought with great distinction in Italy) but was hospitalized due to illness and unable to go. Eddie told me he served in occupied Germany after the war and "had a good time," which seems incongruous with the situation unless there were opportunities for drinking beer and chasing fräulein. It would've been a tremendous irony if he witnessed any of the German concentration camps while he was there.

Eddie's two best friends from the Army (nicknamed "Slim" and "Boots;" one was named Louie, but I don't know their full names) were from St. Louis, Missouri, and that's where he ended up after his military service, working as a groundskeeper for a university. He must've found other opportunities, for his father Tom and the rest of Imada family soon followed him to St. Louis from the Denver area, where they'd settled after release from the internment camp in summer 1945. Eddie's sisters Carolyn and Beverly were born in St. Louis.

The whole family moved back to Colorado early in the 1950s. Tom worked on a truck farm in Denver owned by an Italian American and eventually had his own truck farm in Thornton, now part of metropolitan Denver. Around 1962–63, everyone but Eddie moved to Los Angeles, whence the family'd been so suddenly and unpleasantly evicted 20 years before. Eddie stayed in Thornton.

Chapter 5 – The Courier dojo

Having to do randori nightly with thirty or so partners proved to be quite an arduous task for me. I used to leave for the dojo after an early dinner and arrive back home late, sometimes well after 11 p.m. Because my legs hurt so much following the hard training and exercise sessions, I had difficulty walking in a straight line and occasionally stumbled and fell down.

—Jigoro Kano, ca. 1881, in *Judo Memoirs of Jigoro Kano* by Brian N. Watson, Trafford Publishing, 2008

Eddie started his first class just as Sammy had. We bowed in and did warm-up exercises and ukemi. Rather than lead the exercises himself, he designated one of us to lead, and this became standard practice. He then asked what throws we knew and had pairs of us demonstrate them. The first several pairs demonstrated their throws walking back and forth, as we'd learned.

Finally Eddie stopped the ongoing pair. "Why are you guys walking back and forth like that? No one ever moves that way in judo."

"Well, that's how Sammy showed us to do it," one of us said.

"Huh—that's about what I'd expect from an F.O.B.," Eddie said. F.O.B. (with each letter pronounced individually), meaning "fresh off the boat," was how he referred to native Japanese.

"In judo," Eddie said, "you're never walking strictly back and forth, so it doesn't make sense to practice that way. You need to move this way and that, to get your opponent off balance." We never again practiced throws walking back and forth.

Eddie proceeded to show us the basic stances and ways of moving your feet to maintain balance as you move backward, forward, sideways, or diagonally. He showed us the always-changing equilateral triangle we had to be aware of, whose base is the line between your opponent's feet and whose apex is the direction you need to pull him to put him maximally off balance. He showed us how to grip with the thumb and bottom two fingers, leaving the index and middle fingers loose so that the arms remain flexible. These were all fundamental principles Sammy hadn't elaborated. In Sammy's defense, they might've only confused us as utter beginners, but Eddie realized we weren't utter beginners anymore.

Gradually in the months that followed, Eddie established the class routine we'd follow for the next four years. After we bowed in, warmed up, and practiced ukemi, he explained and demonstrated one or two throws, new or review, and we paired up and practiced them. When there were beginners—and there usually were—he'd delegate a more-advanced student to teach them ukemi.

Then we'd do uchikomi, practicing the techniques we'd just learned as well as favorite throws we were each trying to perfect. In uchikomi, tori can ask for varying degrees of resistance, from none at all, to uke stiffening his trunk and arms, to having a third person hold uke's belt in back, in which case tori can engage with as much force as he can muster.

Another, more intense way we practiced standing techniques was to throw our partner ten times as fast as we could with whatever technique we were working on. Then we switched, and he reciprocated. This went back and forth as long as we could stand it. If it seemed too easy, we could ask our partner to offer some resistance.

Following uchikomi, we did mat work. Mat work is basically wrestling, with the goal of controlling your opponent with his back on the mat using an accepted technique for a set period—in those days, 30 seconds to win the match (in freestyle wrestling, a pin of only 1 second wins the match). There are several basic pinning techniques and variants of each. In addition to the pins, we learned and practiced how to break our opponent out of a defensive prone position, segue form one pinning technique to another to maintain control, escape in the unfortunate event we ourselves were pinned, and avoid getting pinned in the first place.

One way Eddie had us practice mat work was to start with one person solidly pinning his partner, and at the "go" signal, the partner tried to escape. A variation of this was for the pinner to transition from one pin to another while his partner tried to escape. We also did mat-work randori, in which partners sat back to back, and at the "go" signal, turned and tried to pin one another.

Another exercise was to start with one partner in the supine position, his back on his mat, and the other standing. It might seem that the standing partner has an immense advantage, but surprisingly this is not the case. With his back to the mat, the bottom guy has more leverage—he can grip his opponent's lapels and use his own legs to shove his opponent's legs back and out from under him, at the same time rolling him over and ending up on top in a controlling position.

While judo mat work differs from wrestling in the amount of time pins must be held and in the superior gripping opportunities provided by the gi, some pins are similar between the two sports, as are the principles of leverage and balance on the ground. Alamosa was a strong wrestling town at both the high-school and college levels, and some judo-club members were wrestlers who used judo as their off-season training. This was good, for having to contend with their superior skills greatly improved the abilities of the rest of us.

After mat work, we did randori, or free practice. Randori isn't competition; it's most effective with give and take. You assume the basic natural posture rather than stiffer, defensive postures. You engage with people bigger or better than you as well as those smaller or less experienced. If you're with a weaker opponent, you let him throw if he executes a good technique you'd normally be able to evade. You attempt throws other than your favorites, knowing you may well be countered.

You have nothing to lose in randori, for no one's keeping score. Your worst enemy is not your opponent, but your own ego freezing you into a defensive stance, reducing your ability to attack and thus to experiment.

Typically we changed randori partners every 10 minutes or so. Eddie also participated. He could easily throw us at will and did so frequently. Sometimes he let the juniors throw him, but never the high-school students and older. A familiar saying in judo is, "A thousand falls for every throw." This means that you really learn only by practicing with people better than you, which entails getting thrown by them.

Toward the end of every lesson, and this is something I believe led to rapid progress in competition, Eddie staged a mini-shiai (tournament) of 3-minute, all-out matches, with him serving as referee. For the matches, he selected pairs of opponents or took volunteers, sometimes using a "winner stay on" format in which winners continued until they were defeated. Besides providing an outlet that reduced our tendency to go all out in randori, these mini-matches were great for morale.

↜

All beginners in judo endure a toughening-up process. One of the most basic throws in judo is deashi-harai (advanced-foot sweep). It's frequently used as a feint to distract your opponent from some other throw you want to attempt. To properly execute this throw, you sweep a straight leg with your ankle turned inward and catch your opponent's ankle with the fleshy bottom of your foot, just as his weight is going onto or coming off his leg. Imagine someone walking with crutches, and you kick one crutch away just as he's going to put his weight on it. That's deashi-harai.

A successful deashi-harai requires form and timing. Beginners lack the necessary control and frequently hit their opponent's still-grounded leg full force in the shin or calf with a bony part of their foot. Our first year in judo, our shins and outer calves were covered with painful bruises that only became more painful as people hit them repeatedly.

Later we learned how to avoid and counter footsweeps and didn't get hit as much, but our legs also toughened up so that hits no longer hurt. Likewise, in mat work, the arms and legs took a lot abuse rubbing against the gi or mat, and beginners were subject to painful "mat burns." With time, wrists, elbows, knees, and ankles became toughened, and mat burns ceased to be a problem.

↜

When he came to us, Eddie was in superb physical condition. Toughened by daily work gardening and farming and by years of training at the Denver School, he was strong for his size. Various hip and hand throws require the thrower to pivot in to his opponent with knees bent, and to lift the opponent off balance by straightening the knees. Eddie stressed the necessity of strong legs, and to illustrate this point one day—okay, he was showing off a bit—he got an elementary schooler onto each of his shoulders and did several full squats from the standing position.

His first year in Alamosa, Eddie lived the lonely life of a warrior monk. He had little in common with his coworkers at Adams State and initially knew no one else outside the judo club. In summer, he started his workday at 7 AM to minimize exposure to the heat, got off at 4 PM, had dinner, and taught judo in the evening. His lessons were highly organized. He had several well-thumbed judo references at home and studied them before he went to bed to review the finer points of the techniques he intended to teach the next day.

Events in 1963 involved matters small and large. During my first spring in Alamosa, John and Ed Reese and I carried a rubber raft three-quarters of a mile down River Road from our neighborhood, launched it into the Rio Grande, and drifted a couple miles downriver. There were few trees along that stretch of river as it meandered its way south, and we had a clear view of the snowcapped Sangre de Cristos far off across the desert to the northeast. The air was so crystal clear it felt as though a sharp tap'd shatter it. Along the way were occasional old, abandoned homesteads from intrepid souls who'd learned the Valley wasn't entirely the opportunity-filled paradise the real-estate companies'd advertised.

The day was warm enough that shirts were uncomfortable, and we doffed them for our whole time on the river—maybe 5 hours in all. Our backs and arms were red when we left the river, and I thought nothing of it. Over the next few days, however, I had a Chernobyl experience: due to the effects of UV radiation at high elevation, my whole back blistered and then entirely shed its skin in big patches. For the next week or two, judo practices were excruciating, and I had to wear two T-shirts under my gi to minimize the chafing. You'd think once'd be enough, but we did the same thing again the following year.

President Kennedy was assassinated in November 1963. Like everyone else, I remember exactly where I was when I heard the news—in my case, home in bed with the flu. When Jack Ruby shot Lee Harvey Oswald, I remember saying, "Good! He got what he deserved." My mother replied, "No, it's not good at all! Now we'll never know for sure who shot the President—or why." Prophetic words, those.

That fall, the judo club was still in the high school wrestling room. One evening, Takamatsu Sensei from the Denver School and two of his black-belt competitors, Jack Oliver and Leroy Abe, stopped by to see how Eddie was faring, arriving near the end of a practice. It was roughly a year since we'd started judo. The Denver guys were in a hurry and didn't stay long; they were driving to a tournament in Texas and had lost time diverting through Alamosa. We fledgling judoka were immensely impressed; it was like King Arthur riding through with two of his Knights.

In December, Judge Myers formally registered what we loosely called the "judo club" as a nonprofit organization named the San Luis Valley Judo Club. Robert J. "Bob" Bowers became the club president and my mother, Martha M. Dick, the secretary. Bob's connection to judo was that his 7-year-old daughter Toni was in the club. Born in 1929 in Springfield, Massachusetts, he met a Valley woman, Josephine Crow, who was working as a nurse in Denver, and married her in 1948. After the Bowerses returned to the Valley, Bob became a health inspector for the State of Colorado. His main job was to inspect migrant labor camps throughout the Valley to ensure proper sanitary conditions. Farmers didn't like to see him coming, for usually he cost them money, requiring them to erect proper housing with adequate bathing and toilet facilities for their Mexican laborers.

Bob was outspoken and had a notoriously sharp wit. An example was a farmer's wife who accosted him in a supermarket. "Why should we have to spend money to build a mansion with a bathroom for a bunch of damn Mexicans, anyway?" she asked.

Bob replied, "Ma'am, if those workers don't have proper toilet facilities, where do you think they're going to urinate and defecate?" She looked at him blankly, so he held up a head of lettuce to make his point.

Bob made a good president for the judo club. He traveled widely in his job and interacted with farmers, the court system, law enforcement, and local officials. He was also involved in the American Legion. He thus knew a lot of people, and when the judo club needed something—like space for a dojo—he knew whose arm to twist to get it.

My mother, Martha Dick, born in 1921 in Oklahoma, was a woman of many talents. In 1942, she earned a BA degree in anthropology from the University of New Mexico, where she met my father. When I was in grade school in Trinidad, she went back to school, obtained a teaching certificate, and taught high-school algebra. In Alamosa, she took calculus and other math classes at Adams State, for what purpose I don't know. I remember sitting at the kitchen table with her when I was in 9th grade, she doing her homework and I doing mine. Her pursuit of further education in Alamosa was interrupted when she started a bookstore. After that closed, she did tax returns for H & R Block. Some summers, she served as camp cook for my father's archaeological field schools. In conjunction with the field schools, she undertook first-aid training and later became a volunteer EMT (emergency medical technician) in Alamosa.

Martha's lifelong passion was volunteerism; when there was a civic job that needed doing, she jumped in—for example, PTA president and

Cub Scout mother in Trinidad; judo club secretary and EMT in Alamosa. With her math skills, keeping the judo club's accounts was child's play.

↩

When the Judge incorporated the judo club, he also designed and had professionally produced a cloth insignia patch for us to sew onto the right breast of our judo gi. We stenciled our surname on the left breast.

In the shape of an equilateral parallelogram, wider than tall, our insignia had a black border and white background, with an inner parallelogram also bordered in black. Around the edges of the inner field was written, left to right and top to bottom, SAN LUIS – VALLEY JUDO – CLUB OF – COLORADO. **[Illustration, p. 153]** Horizontal within the inner field in green stitching were four snowcapped mountain peaks with a perspective grid of farm fields beneath them, representing Sangre de Cristo range and San Luis Valley. Above, in the sky, like a sun rising over the mountains, was the judo symbol.

The judo symbol looks like an eight-petaled flower with a red circle in the center. The flower outline, however, actually represents an octagonal copper mirror, the yata-kagami, with deep mythological and religious significance in Japan as one of three items that passed from the Gods to the first Emperor. As mirrors truthfully reflect images, the mirror signifies honesty. The red circle inside represents an iron core and the white background, soft silk. The idea of the judo symbol is "hard inner core, gentle external demeanor."

↩

In November or December 1963, we thankfully moved from the high school to the first dojo we could call our own. This was a single-story retail building with big storefront windows, located on the corner of Fourth and State in downtown Alamosa. The building was for sale or rent but'd been vacant for a while. I doubt we could've afforded to rent it with dues money as our only source of income, so I suspect either Bob Bowers or the Judge managed to get it at a discount or for free, perhaps by convincing the owner to donate its use as a tax write-off. I'll refer to this place as the Courier building, because the *Valley Courier*, a local newspaper, occupied it either before or after we were there.

Traditionally, the practice area in a judo dojo is covered with tatami mats laid edge to edge, each about 3 feet by 6 feet in dimensions and roughly 2 inches thick. Still used as floor covering in homes in Japan, tatami originally consisted of a finely woven fabric of natural rushes covering an inner core of tightly sewn rice straw.

Today, thicker mats of similar dimensions and appearance are manufactured specifically for martial-arts practice, but instead of incorporating natural materials, these have a layered foam core with a tatami-textured vinyl covering. Tatami were and are expensive. Top quality, 2-inch-thick, 3-by-6-foot tatami for judo now retail for about $150 apiece. A 30-foot by 30-foot practice area requires 50 standard-sized tatami that would cost $7500 at today's prices.

Prices were less in 1963 than now, but so was everything else, including dues fees. There was no way we could've afforded tatami for our dojo. Judge Myers did some research and found a cheaper, do-it-yourself solution that involved constructing a wooden frame 18 inches high around the periphery of the practice area, anchoring it to the floor with stout L-brackets, filling it with sawdust, and covering the sawdust with a single expanse of white, heavy-duty canvas. This is what we did, although I only vaguely remember helping with it.

We inaugurated the new dojo on a Saturday early in January 1964, though we may've already moved there some weeks earlier. A short news article in the newspaper *Rocky Mountain JIHO* on 8 January 1964 noted that Takamatsu Sensei'd arranged for Ken and Yo Fushimi, a Mr. Hall, and 16 students from the Denver School to travel to Alamosa to participate in the inauguration. The article ended with, "About 50 students from valley communities will practice four nights weekly." This shows how much we'd grown in a little over a year, and that if we weren't already practicing four nights a week, we soon would be. I believe we met Mondays through Thursdays for practices 3 hours long, 7–10 PM.

By the time we got to the Courier building, we had a broader age range, from grade school to college, including girls and women. I vaguely remember that at this time, Eddie taught a kids' class 7–8 PM and then an adults' class 8–10 PM. Practices were crowded, though not all club members showed up every evening. A quirk of the dojo was that the sawdust in the mat shifted around and packed unevenly, developing humps and hollows. Every few weeks, we had to draw back the canvas and level the sawdust.

While we were in the Courier building, Lieutenant Lawrence Martinez of the Alamosa Police Department periodically used the dojo as the venue for teaching women's self-defense classes he called "Dirty Street Fighting." This might seem to go against Sammy Tahara's admonitions against judoka engaging in street fighting, but not really. The Lieutenant would've agreed that one shouldn't willfully engage in street fighting, and that judo wasn't particularly effective for this purpose. He'd have argued, however, that in dire situations of self-defense, it was best to fight fire with fire—that a swift knee to the testicles or stomp to the instep served much better than attempting a judo throw against a violent aggressor.

Located downtown, the Courier building was close to a number of bars and restaurants. At first, passersby on their way home'd stand in the cold in front of the big retail display windows to watch us practice. Pretty soon they began filtering in and standing just inside the door. This created an inconvenient jam-up around the door, so the Judge finally brought in folding chairs to accommodate both the rubberneckers and parents waiting to pick up their kids.

Before we knew it, we had spectators in various states of inebriation from various walks of life—farmers, college students, businessmen, housewives—watching judo. This was never a problem; in fact, it was the best advertising we could've had, for I'm sure we attracted new members from it. Furthermore, Eddie was soon a minor celebrity; people'd occasionally stop him on the street or in stores, "Excuse me, but aren't you that guy who teaches judo downtown?"

Sometime that winter, we put on a judo demonstration at the American Legion hall. Judo demonstrations were always a big hit. The thrower looks tremendously skilled because the faller offers no resistance at all. The breakfall makes such a loud noise that it appears bones are being broken. It's perfect showmanship.

The Judge had mats transported to the venue, but we changed to our judo gi at the Courier building and went on foot to the demonstration. I remember 10 or so of us in judo gi and street shoes, jogging along the sidewalk because it was cold. It was a Saturday afternoon and the town was busy. A farmer driving by in a beat-up pickup did a double take and slowed down to watch a bunch of kids running by in their pajamas, probably thinking, "What the hell?" Among us were the Kelso brothers—stout, blond farm boys from one of the small towns like Center or Hooper, in grade school but big for their ages—skipping along, laughing and hooting, loving it.

The following spring, the Alamosa-La Jara Japanese Association asked us to stage a similar demonstration at the Buddhist Church in La Jara. This may've come about because a pair of Japanese brothers from La Jara, Nobu and Satsu Yoshida, were in the judo club. We had a good turnout of

Japanese people from all over the Valley. No one had to transport mats for that demonstration, because the church already had tatami.

Chapter 6 – Competition

The rules governing current competitive judo seem to have adversely influenced the posture that many pupils adopt when engaged not only in contest but also in their regular randori bouts in the dojo.

—Jigoro Kano, in *Judo Memoirs of Jigoro Kano* by Brian N. Watson, Trafford Publishing, 2008

When I started judo, I knew so little about the sport I didn't even realize competitions existed—though why wouldn't they? The first tournament we attended was in Albuquerque in the fall of 1963, a month or two before we moved to the Courier building. None of us'd been in judo for more than a year, some of us less.

Since this was my first competitive event in any sport, I should remember the overall experience better than I do. What stands out in my mind is largely negative. The sensei of the Albuquerque club seemed to put his self-respect on the line for each of his students' matches. In short, he was a screamer, kneeling at the sideline and shouting loud, obnoxious encouragement and advice. It was undignified and in stark contrast to Eddie, who was stoic and silent. Eddie might offer advice before a match or point out mistakes afterward, but once it was underway, he left us alone. Shouted advice was irrelevant to me, for I completely tuned out crowd noise.

In the Albuquerque tournament, Kent Myers, who like the rest of us was still a white belt, beat the Albuquerque sensei's teenaged son, who was a purple belt. At the end of the tournament, seemingly to save face, the Albuquerque sensei protested vehemently to Eddie that Kent shouldn't be competing as a white belt and promoted him on the spot to 3rd-kyu purple belt (more about ranks later). Eddie certainly would've had some say in the matter, and apparently he agreed. In any case, Kent was the first SLV judoka to reach colored-belt rank.

The Albuquerque sensei may've behaved as he did partly because he had a commercial school and taught judo as a means of making a livelihood, or at least a profit. There's nothing wrong with this, if the instructor's qualified and able in this way to maintain a dojo. But the Albuquerque sensei may've felt it was not good advertising when a new club working out in substandard conditions in a small town came to the City and defeated at least one of his star players—hence his rabid kibitzing.

↜

Though we might not've known initially that we were headed toward competition, Eddie did and began preparing us soon after he got to Alamosa.

In addition to the basic throws, he taught combinations, where one throw, if unsuccessful, nonetheless sets your opponent off balance for a different one. Two techniques particularly effective in combinations are the major (ouchi-gari) and minor (kouchi-gari) inner reaping throws. These are simple to visualize. Imagine facing your opponent, who has his legs spread somewhat apart. In right-handed ouchi-gari, you move your right leg between his legs and hook your right calf against his nearest (his left) calf, pulling his leg toward you and tripping him backwards. Kouchi-gari is similar; you move your right leg between his legs but catch your opponent's opposite (his right) leg at the ankle with your foot and sweep his leg forward, likewise throwing him backward.

These throws might be successful in themselves. To avoid them, your opponent has to get his leg out of the way by raising it up and back, and this puts him off balance forward, making him vulnerable to a virtual treasure trove of forward throws. Conversely, if you try a forward throw and your opponent shifts his balance backward to avoid it, he becomes vulnerable to ouchi- and kouchi-gari.

You can't learn all throws equally well, and which ones you focus on will depend partly on your body form. For example, if you're short and stout, you'll have an advantage in executing techniques that require you to pivot in low to your opponent with bent legs, using your buttocks against his thighs as the fulcrum for the throw—examples are seoi-nage (shoulder throw) and tsurikomi-goshi (lift-pull hip throw).

On the other hand, if you're tall and long-legged, you want to focus on techniques where you don't need to bend your legs so deeply, and can even keep one of them straight as you use it in a sweeping motion. I have long legs and feet and thus favored footsweeps, harai-goshi (hip sweep), uchi-mata (inner-thigh reaping throw), and ouchi-gari and kouchi-gari mentioned above, for which long legs are an advantage.

In the end, it's best to perfect at least one throw of each type, for whether you are tall or short, you'll occasionally encounter opponents even taller or shorter. While uchi-mata might work on most opponents, it won't work well on a taller one, where seoi-nage might work better.

In addition to combinations, Eddie taught us counters for various standing throws. For example, to counter a footsweep, you can bend the target leg up at the knee so the sweep misses altogether, instantly coming around with your own footsweep, taking advantage of your opponent's foot already moving in the right direction. This counter greatly reduced the incidence of frivolous footsweeps.

Early on, we learned ura-nage (back throw), a brutal counter for an opponent who's pivoted in for a throw and has his back to you. You wrap your arms around him, firmly binding him to you, and fall backward with a twist, hurling him down behind you. This is potentially dangerous, and you need to take care your opponent doesn't land on his head. Sooner or later, virtually everyone lands badly with ura-nage and has his breath knocked out.

Once every week or two, to break up the routine, Eddie drew a large circle on the mat with a piece of chalk and had us doff our gi jackets to engage in sumo bouts. The rules of sumo are entirely different from those in judo; you win when your opponent touches the mat with any part of his body other than his feet or steps outside the circle. Because there's no jacket, there's little except the belt to grasp, so sumo requires meticulous attention to balance—both yours and your opponent's. It's extremely useful cross-training for judo.

Another training method Eddie instituted later on was blind randori, where one partner closes his eyes. The other keeps his open to avoid running into other randori pairs or going off the mat. Not seeing isn't as big a disadvantage as you might expect. After a year or two of experience, it's easy to sense where your opponent's legs are and where he'll move them when you attempt to pull him off balance. Blind randori greatly sharpens awareness of your opponent's "telegraphing"—that is, indicating by subtle, unintended body movements what throw he intends to use.

ᔇ

Competitive judo between skilled, evenly matched opponents can be boring to watch, even if you know what's going on. Opponents will have solid stances that are difficult to penetrate, and they continually struggle for favored grips. They attempt throws that their opponent sees coming and easily deflects. One opponent'll get knocked to the ground and the other'll attempt to pin him. If there's no progress in a reasonable time, the referee breaks it up. Matches can go to the end in this humdrum manner, with the judges and referee eventually deciding the winner (matches are decided differently now but can still be humdrum to the end).

You can't take your eyes off this tedium for a second, however, because every so often someone slips up and is thrown instantly and perfectly. The loser lands hard on his back, knowing without a doubt he's just lost. It's exciting. It's poetry. It's like seeing an exquisite orchid suddenly blooming from a pile of dung.

ᔇ

The rules for competitive judo were different in the 1960s than they are now, and an examination of the rules then and changes to them over the years will give some insight into competition. When SLV Judo began, the rules for US national competition were set by the AAU (Amateur Athletic Union) in coordination with the JBBF (Judo Black Belt Federation).

In judo, you need only one point to win. Under traditional rules, a clean throw that lands your opponent on his back with speed, force, and control is awarded ippon (one point), and the match is over. A throw that lacks one of these elements is scored as waza-ari (a certain amount of technique). Waza-ari is valued at a half-point and is cumulative, so that you can win by scoring two waza-ari.

You can also win by holding your opponent under control with a recognized pinning technique. In the 1960s, a pin of 30 seconds was required for ippon and 25 seconds for waza-ari.

There are two other ways to win a match. One is by successful application of a choke hold. You win by ippon when your opponent taps several times with his hand or foot to signal submission, or the referee judges he's about to black out. Contestants 12 years old and under aren't allowed to use choke holds in competition.

Another is by successful application of an arm bar, where your opponent "taps out" or gives up verbally. Arm bars are tricky because there's a fine line between causing enough pain to force submission and damaging your opponent's joint. They're allowed in competition only against black-belt ranks, under the reasoning that only black belts have enough experience to avoid injury.

In the 1960s, each match had a referee and two judges. The judges sat in chairs at two corners of the contest area, whereas the referee (as now) moved around as the players moved. Both competitors wore a white judo gi. To assist the judges and referee in telling them apart, each tied a long cloth ribbon to his belt, either red or white, with the ends dangling. The two judges each had a red flag and a white flag. If a match came to a decision, each judge'd raise the flag indicating his choice for winner. In the case of a judges' tie, the referee had the deciding vote, after conferring with the judges.

According to the 1963 rule book, early-round matches in AAU "Olympic-style" tournaments were 6 minutes long, with one 5-minute overtime permitted. Matches in semifinal and final rounds were 10 minutes long, with two 5-minute overtimes permitted. Draws weren't allowed in individual competition. After the set number of overtime periods, a judges' decision had to be rendered. Matches in non-AAU tournaments could be shorter at the discretion of the tournament committee, but I don't believe they were ever shorter than 5 minutes. Due to the long match times, referees tended not to break up mat work as quickly as they do now when progress toward an outcome was slow—many referees permitted the contestants to wrestle awhile.

The 1963 rule book listed 22 "prohibited acts," many of which dealt with safety (no leg locks, no striking your opponent, no bending back your opponent's fingers to break his grip, etc.) or unfair advantage (overly defensive grips or postures; no grabbing your opponent's sleeves or pants by inserting your fingers into the ends, etc.). It was also prohibited to grab your opponent's leg from the standing position solely to force him into mat work.

When a competitor committed a prohibited act, the referee charged him with a formal violation of the rules (hansoku). At a second violation, the referee awarded a waza-ari to his opponent. I believe violations were rare; I don't recall ever being cited for one. Referees were encouraged to warn competitors before penalizing them. In mat work, it's illegal to place your hand on your opponent's face to force him away, and I remember instances of a referee stepping in and physically batting away an offending hand rather than calling a violation.

Perhaps due to the growth of judo and increasing number of competitors, one trend in rules changes had to do with reducing the lengths of matches and overtimes. Over the years, match times were reduced to 5 and then 4 minutes. Pin times necessary for ippon and waza-ari were each reduced by 5 seconds, from 30 and 25 seconds to 25 and 20 seconds.

To reduce presumed subjectivity in judges' decisions, two scores lower than waza-ari (yuko and koka) were added to the rules in 1975. Recall that the score of ippon (one point) is awarded for throws that land the opponent on his back with control, force, and speed, and waza-ari (half-point) for throws lacking one of these elements. The yuko score became available for throws lacking two of these elements or a pin lasting 15 to 19 seconds before being broken. A koka was awarded for a throw that had speed and force but landed the opponent on his shoulder, hip, or stomach, or a pin of 10 to 14 seconds.

In the 1980s, the scoring system in judo amounted to a Rube Goldberg apparatus of impressive proportions. In conjunction with the introduction of the yuko and koka scores, prohibited acts were intricately subdivided into four categories—shido (slight), chui (serious), keikoku (grave), and hansoku-make (very grave)—with rules for converting cumulative lower penalties to higher ones. Thus, for example, two shido converted to chui; chui and another shido to keikoku; keikoku and any other penalty to hansoku-make.

At the end of the contest, penalties accumulated by one opponent converted to scores for the other: a shido penalty to a koka score, a chui to a yuko score, and a keikoku to waza-ari. Cumulative koka scores didn't convert to yuko, nor cumulative yuko scores to waza-ari, but a difference of one koka could decide the match at the end, all else being equal.

Refereeing and scorekeeping under this onerous system must've been a flaming nightmare. One thing this minute parsing of scores and penalties apparently accomplished was to eliminate overtimes, of which I can find no mention in the 1985 IJF (International Judo Federation) rules. Apparently, in the unlikely event of a draw, opponents had the option to refight the match from the beginning.

Another trend in rules changes had to do with making judo more pleasing to spectators by reducing the time spent in mat work—there was a growing feeling that judo was becoming "wrestling in pajamas." With shorter match times, referees tended to break up mat work quicker if no resolution was in sight.

To reduce the ways a competitor might take his opponent to the mat, touching or gripping his thighs or legs below the belt while standing became prohibited. This had other consequences as well; for example, an effective way to block an opponent's hip throw was simply to push his hip away with your hand. This became illegal, if you pushed below the belt.

Mat techniques remained important, and indeed many judoka continued to practice mat work as intensively as standing techniques. Competitors just had to become faster and more effective in controlling their opponents after aborted and non-scoring throws, and in scoring with pins, chokes, and arm bars. At the very least, it remained important to avoid being pinned, for escaping from pins takes immense energy and can detrimentally exhaust the escapee in the process.

While a few techniques such as kani-basami (scissors throw) and kawazu-gake) (one-leg entanglement) had been banned because they tended to cause injury, the no-touching-below-the-belt rule effectively banned several other relatively safe throws that involved grabbing one or both of your opponent's legs. Several of these look suspiciously like standard takedowns used in wrestling and could effectively serve as such, even if they were sloppily done and didn't result in a point. Morote-gari (the two-handed reap), for instance, is basically a front tackle of the legs. Kata-guruma (the shoulder wheel) is very similar to the fireman's-carry takedown in wrestling.

Let's fast forward to 2021 and compare the situation with the 1960s, when there were longer matches and discrete overtime periods, fewer restrictions on gripping, fewer restricted throws, and a simpler scoring system. The koka score was abolished in 2008 and the yuko score in 2017, so these're no longer considerations.

Instead of wearing red or white ribbons tied to their belts, one contestant now wears a blue gi and the other a white one. Judges no longer sit at the corners of the contest area but at a table off one side of the mat, where one or more video cameras connected to laptop computers allow instant replay. An electronic scoreboard shows points, penalties, and time.

Initial Olympic-style matches are now 4 minutes long. You can win with a technical score (ippon or waza-ari), or lose by disqualification. Violations are categorized simply as minor (shido) or major (hansoku make). Many of the minor penalties established in the old days have been retained, but there's been a proliferation of rules having to do with grips, the no-leg-touching rule previously mentioned, stalling, overly defensive posture, and what defines the transition from standing rules to mat rules.

As before, the major violations exist largely to prevent injury, to either the thrower or the faller. For example, if you're the thrower, it's illegal to dive forward with your opponent on your back when you're attempting a hip or shoulder throw. Likewise, if you're the faller, it's forbidden to land in a "bridge" position on your head and toes to avoid landing on your back. These rules are intended to prevent head and neck injuries and result in your losing the match, either as thrower or faller.

Recall that in the old days, if you were cited for rule violations, your opponent was awarded a waza-ari. Penalties no longer convert to points in this manner. If you receive a major violation, you're disqualified and lose the match. A further little quirk is that three minor violations convert to a major one, and you lose the match just as if you'd committed a single major violation.

An overtime again exists in competition. It has no time limit and is called the "golden score period," because the match goes to first person who wins with a technical score (ippon or waza-ari), or whose opponent loses by hansoku-make. All points and shido penalties from the 4-minute regulation period continue into the golden score period. So, for example, if both opponents go into golden score with a waza-ari and two shido penalties, the first to get another waza-ari or an ippon wins, or the first to accumulate a third shido through a minor violation loses, by the rule converting three shido to hansoku-make.

The criteria for scoring've been watered down. "Rolling ippon" are permitted, for example, where the faller doesn't come down hard onto his back but is rolled onto it. Many of the rolling-ippon scores seen now would've been called waza-ari in the 1960s. Waza-ari was redefined to include landings previously awarded yuko scores. Now, you can score waza-ari if your opponent lands on his side without his back touching at all, or if he lands on his butt, with his back raised from the mat—things that wouldn't have scored at all in the old days.

In a cryptic and seemingly self-contradictory statement, the 2021 IJF rulebook states, "In order not to give a bad example for young judokas, landing on both elbows or two hands, simultaneously, or one elbow and one hand, is considered valid and should be evaluated with waza-ari."

It's unclear how awarding a half-point for such grossly inadequate throws is a good example of anything. Inserting "not" before "considered" and "be" would make more sense.

There's always been a struggle for favored grips in judo matches. Now, however, this struggle reaches manic proportions, as if allowing your opponent to grip at all with both hands will automatically lead to his throwing you and your loss of the match. It's not uncommon to see competitors with all their fingertips taped due to wear and tear in the struggle for grips, something I don't remember seeing in the old days.

Some contestants behave like wrestlers, circling one another with no grip at all, seeking the opportunity to dash in for a favorable grip. I timed several televised women's matches in the 2020 (2021) Tokyo Olympics, and in two of them, the contestants didn't touch one another at all for between one-quarter and one-third of the match! It's damned hard to throw someone if you aren't touching the person, but on the other hand, you can't be thrown either.

This maneuvering without touching amounts to stalling and is technically a violation, but what's a referee to do? The ref could penalize both non-touching opponents repeatedly with simultaneous shido calls, but both would rapidly accumulate three shido and be disqualified from the match at the same time. The match'd end in a draw, which isn't permissible. The same considerations apply when both contestants assume an overly defensive posture for prolonged periods.

In some matches, the strategy now seems to be avoiding getting thrown during the regulation match period, putting in the appearance of just enough effort to avoid shido calls for stalling. You then put in slightly more effort than your opponent during the golden score period so that he or she draws a third shido before you and loses the match by default. Some players seem to have developed only one technique and attempt it repeatedly, "telegraphing" when they do this, so their opponent can easily avoid it. But this apparently counts as "effort."

This cynical portrayal of current judo isn't universal. The best players engage with a style that the Japanese refer to as "beautiful judo." They maintain a relatively erect posture, grip more continuously, and quickly execute a throw after momentarily achieving a favorable grip. They use a variety of techniques, combinations, and counters, right and left, to create openings and take advantage of opponents' mistakes. I believe that Jigoro Kano would've been disgusted by the worst of modern judo but elated by the best of it.

Chapter 7 – Intense season

Judo rank should be kept as a reward in fighting and coaching. ... We aren't in any race with each other for the prestige of rank. We don't attach community position to judo rank. Most of us are in judo for the fighting-coaching activities involved rather than the social prestige, if indeed there is any in our American [judo] *communities.*

—Jim Bregman, in "Friction Fractures U.S. Judo Factions," *Black Belt Magazine* 1970, 8(6), p. 26.

Once we'd started competing, we soon learned there was no shortage of shiai (fighting tournaments) in the Rocky Mountain region. These were organized in various ways—by age, weight, a combination of age and weight, or rank.

By age, competitors were considered to be juniors (ages 6 to 16) or seniors (17 and older). Juniors could further be subdivided into yonen (kids; aged 12 and under) and shonen (intermediates, aged 13 to 16). Some junior tournaments had a separate division for each age from 6 to 16, totaling 11 divisions. In the junior Olympic format, there were four age groups—midget ($\leq$10 years), junior (11–12 years), intermediate (13–14 years), and senior (in this context, 15–16 years)—each of which was divided into light (the lighter half of the contestants) and heavy (heavier half) divisions. There were thus eight divisions defined by age and weight.

In senior tournaments (age 17 and older), divisions were based on weight in specified intervals, for example $\leq$135 lb, $\leq$150 lb, $\leq$165 lb, $\leq$180 lb, $\leq$195 lb, and >195 lb (unlimited). AAU national, regional, and Olympic-development tournaments had only three weight divisions: $\leq$150 lb, $\leq$176 lb, and >176 lb (unlimited).

A general rule allowed contestants to compete in an age or weight division higher than they were eligible for, if they chose, which meant that intermediates (ages 13 to 16) could compete in senior tournaments. During 1964, our first full competitive season, many of us in the SLV Judo Club were intermediates and provided good warm-up fodder for older, more experienced opponents in senior tournaments.

Some tournaments were structured around rank, and to understand these, it is necessary first to understand the ranking system. The basic division in rank is between students (designated "kyu") and teachers ("dan"). In Kodokan ranking, the oldest and only internationally recognized system, there are six ranks for kyu and 12 for dan.

The numbering systems for kyu and dan run in opposite directions: kyu ranks range from absolute beginner (6th kyu) through experienced student (1st kyu), whereas dan ranks range from the lowest (1st dan) to the highest (12th dan). In everyday usage, Japanese numbers are prefixed to the ranks; for example, 3nd kyu is called sankyu, 3rd dan is called sandan, etc. To avoid confusion, I'll use the Arabic numerals.

The only person to have held 12th-dan rank was Jigoro Kano, the founder of judo. For reasons of respect, the maximum rank anyone else can attain is two ranks below that at 10th dan. To date, only 15 men and no women have attained 10th-dan rank recognized by the Kodokan, although some other judo federations have promoted a few people to this level, including one woman. Among the few people to reach Kodokan 10th-dan rank, some were direct students of Jigoro Kano.

Belt colors are used to indicate rank, and this has given rise to a veritable rainbow of colors for kyu ranks in some judo associations around the world. In the relatively simple system at the Denver School of Judo (and, by extension, SLV), ranks from 6th to 4th kyu, regardless of age, wore a white belt. Ranks from 3rd to 1st kyu wore a green belt as juniors (through age 12), a purple belt as intermediates (13–16), and a brown belt as seniors (17 and older). In most systems, 1st-kyu brown belt is the penultimate rank before 1st-dan black belt. The minimum age to attain 1st dan is 15 years.

In a system called "rank conversion," juniors who reach 1st-kyu rank convert to 3rd-kyu purple belt (normally for intermediates), and intermediates who reach 1st kyu convert to 3rd-kyu brown belt (normally for seniors). I attained 3rd-kyu purple-belt rank in 1964 at age 14. Wayne Fushimi, my nemesis early on at the Denver School and roughly the same age as I, attained 3rd-kyu brown belt in May 1963. This means that, depending on his birthday, he became a brown belt at age 13 or 14.

Belts for dan ranks are consistent worldwide. Judoka ranked from 1st to 5th dan wear a black belt; from 6th to 8th dan, a belt colored in alternating segments of red and white; and 9th and 10th dan, a belt of solid red.

Tournaments based on rank included novice tournaments for white belts; brown-belt tournaments for ranks of brown belt and lower; and rank tournaments, with each division comprising a specific rank or range of ranks—for example, 4th kyu and lower (white belts), 3rd kyu, 2nd kyu, 1st kyu, 1st dan, and 2nd dan and above.

In terms of operation, tournaments for individual competitors could be either single or double elimination. In single elimination, if you lost a match, you were out of the tournament. In double elimination, if you lost a match, you went into a losers' pool and had another chance.

A lot of shiai were available in the Rocky Mountain area during the period 1963–1967, when the SLV Judo Club was most active. The Denver School of Judo alone held no fewer than eight from December 1963 to May 1964, our first main competitive season, as follows (Denver organized the same suite of shiai annually). **[Illustration, p. 160]**

Olympic Development Tournament, 15 December 1963. This was primarily for seniors (though intermediates 13 and older also competed) in six weight divisions, ≤135 lb to ≤195 lb in 15-lb intervals and >195 lb (unlimited). There were 51 competitors from the Denver School, Amid of Denver, Colorado State University, University of Colorado, Air Force Academy, and Lowry Air Force Base. SLV did not participate.

Junior Olympic Tournament, 12 January 1964. This tournament had 11 age divisions, from 6 to 16. Over 150 competitors from eight clubs attended, including SLV, the Denver School, Amid of Denver, Boulder Imperial, Brighton, Colorado Springs, Craig, and Lowry Air Force Base. With this number of competitors to handle in a single afternoon, the contest format was single elimination. Three judoka from SLV placed.

Novice Tournament, 9 February 1964. This was for white belts only. Seven Colorado clubs participated, including SLV. While it included intermediates, it also included seniors, because Colorado State University placed 1st in three divisions. I could find no other results.

Brown Belt Tournament, 23 February 1964. This was for intermediates and seniors (age 13 and older), with six weight divisions (≤135 lb to unlimited in 15-lb intervals). SLV didn't yet have any brown belts, so this competition must've been for anyone ranked brown belt and under. A club from Albuquerque and seven Colorado clubs participated, including SLV, but no one from SLV placed.

11th Annual Rocky Mountain Regional Invitational Tournament, 7–8 March 1964. This was the Denver School's premier annual event, a 2-day affair that started on a Saturday afternoon or evening and continued on Sunday. It had seven weight divisions, ≤80 lb to ≤180 lb in 20-lb intervals and >180 lb (unlimited). With the low-weight divisions, it included juniors through seniors. Fourteen clubs participated, mostly from Colorado but also from Cheyenne, Wyoming and Omaha, Nebraska. SLV participated, but none of us placed. The Denver School took 15 of 21 possible places, and 1st place in all but one division.

Rocky Mountain Association AAU Open Championships, 12 April 1964. This was an open senior competition, with six weight divisions in mostly 15-lb intervals, ≤135 lb, ≤150 lb, ≤165 lb, ≤180 lb, ≤200 lb, and >200 lb (unlimited). Six Colorado clubs participated, including SLV, but no one from SLV placed. The Denver School took 14 of 18 places.

Five-Man Team Championships, 26 April 1964. I could find no record of participants or results.

Rank Championships, 17 May 1964. I could find no record of participants or results.

Shiai outside Denver in 1964 included a Junior Olympic Tournament at the Colorado Springs Judo School on 21 June and the "State AAU," probably at Otero Junior College in La Junta, in summer or fall.

⤵

We traveled to tournaments by car. Eddie had an old, white beater station wagon and took as many of us as he could. Judge Myers often drove a car, as did my mother. Back then, with a 55-mph speed limit, it was a 5-hour drive from Alamosa to Denver. Most tournaments were on Sunday, so we'd drive up the Saturday before. This was a touch-and-go proposition in Colorado in the winter; sometimes we got caught in blizzards that made driving slow and treacherous.

My paternal aunt, uncle, and three female cousins—the Pipiringos family—lived in southwest Denver about 5 miles from the Denver School and provided lodging for my mother, me, and any other SLV students who drove with us. We students took along sleeping bags and sacked out on a throw rug in the basement.

I was so nervous before my first few shiai in Denver that I lay awake for most of the night before each of them, paralyzed with misgivings, dreading the next day. I don't know what I was afraid of. I knew how to fall, so injury was unlikely. Furthermore, there was nothing qualitatively different between a tournament match and the 3-minute shiai bouts we did toward the end of every practice. It must've been akin to stage fright, the foreboding that I'd somehow make a fool of myself. This irrational apprehension went away by the time I started placing in tournaments but was distinctly unpleasant while it lasted.

For tournaments with weight classes, we had to be at the Denver School between 9 and 10 AM to weigh in. Junior Olympic Tournaments had age rather than weight divisions, so there was probably no weigh-in, but there would've been a check-in.

Tournaments started at 1 PM, so after weigh-in or check-in, we invariably had an early lunch at the Mandarin Cafe, a couple blocks from the Denver School, where we ordered beef teriyaki and rice. For most of us, the Mandarin was our first encounter with Japanese cuisine and the use of chopsticks. With each meal came a complimentary gelatinous candy named "Tomoe Ame." This candy was wrapped in rice paper, and it seemed astoundingly exotic that we could eat the wrapping.

↩

Our second competition was the Junior Olympic Tournament at the Denver School in January 1964. I was in the 14-year-old division. For my first match, I had the bad luck to draw Wayne Fushimi, a brown belt and the ultimate winner of the division. We danced around for about 20 seconds, whereupon he threw me with tai-otoshi for an ippon, and I was out of the tournament. Kent Myers and Laurier Couture were in the same division; while they might've lasted longer than one match, neither fared any better than I in the end.

For me, a 20-second defeat seemed incredibly little to show for a 10-hour round-trip drive to Denver in winter and a sleepless night worrying. The only consolations were seeing my cousins, lunch at the Mandarin, and stopping for 10-cent hamburgers at an isolated roadside MacDonald's north of Walsenburg.

Our defeats weren't surprising, given that the three winners in the 14-year-old division'd been in judo for 6 to 8 years and competed many times before. In contrast, most of us from SLV had a little over a year under our belts, so to speak, and this was our second tournament.

Encouragingly, three SLV judoka did place: Gary Gallagher 3rd among the 13 year olds, Harry Sumida Jr. 1st among the 8 year olds, and Randy Sumida 3rd among the 7 year olds. Gary was talented and could've gone far but soon quit judo in favor of football. Randy and Harry Jr. may've started judo before any of the rest of us, as their father'd converted a room in their home to a dojo and taught them the basics. They already knew ukemi and various throws when they first attended practices at SLV sometime in 1963.

Wayne Fushimi, who beat me so handily, was a rising star at the Denver School and would've remained a threat. Fortunately for us, he switched his athletic prowess to high-school football and disappeared entirely from the judo scene for the next several years. God, I loved football for that!

⌖

I have a 3rd-place medal labeled "State AAU, 1964, 14 years old." This shiai was somewhere other than the Denver School and took place after the main season, probably in summer or fall. It was the first tournament I placed in. I well remember a string of defeats in five tournaments before finally placing, which means that in a year or less, from fall 1963 (Albuquerque) to summer or fall 1964 (State AAU), I attended six tournaments. SLV Judo Club was represented in at least seven shiai during the same period. I now find it incredible that we were so active in our first competitive season.

Because of conflicting activities, not everyone participated in every tournament. Furthermore, we became ineligible for novice tournaments when we reached colored-belt rank and junior tournaments when we reached age 17. This gradually reduced the number of shiai we could attend. Across the 3.5 years I competed for SLV, I attended 15 or 16 tournaments, averaging over four per year.

Due largely to driving distances in the West, SLV restricted its competition to Colorado and New Mexico—in Colorado, tournaments in Denver, Colorado Springs, the Air Force Academy, Pueblo, La Junta, Craig, and possibly Cortez; in New Mexico, Albuquerque and Roswell.

The Denver School of Judo ranged more widely. For example, in 1964 a large contingent of all ages attended the Invitational Tournament in Ogden, Utah in February. A photo taken upon their return to Denver shows a group 37 people, including competitors, coaches, and parents, bundled in winter coats, with luggage scattered around, indicating they traveled by air. DSJ sent another large contingent to the Intermountain Tournament in Salt Lake City in November. Denver dominated both events.

⌒

Various parts of the world have their odd little sporting events, like Finnish wife carrying or Michigan outhouse racing. In this category in the San Luis Valley was an annual rabbit drive, which I attended with Bob Bowers in the fall of 1964.

The basic premises of the rabbit drive were that there were too many jackrabbits in the Valley; that these were agricultural pests, collectively eating large amounts of crops; and that killing them was thus good. One of the local service organizations, the Lions Club or Rotary, organized the drive and made money by charging an entrance fee as well as selling the resulting rabbit carcasses, either for the pelts or to be used in dog food, or both.

To execute the drive, a hundred or more participants with shotguns ringed the periphery of a large piece of chico-brush-covered land, either a quarter-section or a section (1/2 or 1 mile square). At a start signal, they all began walking toward the center of the property, shouting and whistling as they went, driving rabbits ahead of them. While jackrabbits were rather sparse if you were just out hiking, they became much more concentrated in the shrinking circle of noisy hunters.

The cardinal rule of the drive was that you waited until the rabbits made a break for it, dashing between people to escape, and shot at them outside the circle as they ran away, to avoid shooting people opposite or adjacent to you. There was some action all along as the smarter and braver among the rabbits chose to exit the circle while there was still a lot of space between humans. Even with so many hunters, some of them got away. The jackrabbits zigzagged, disappearing behind clumps of chico and reappearing in unexpected directions. They were so fast you had to lead them, adjusting the lead to the speed and angle at which they were running from you.

Anyone with a shotgun, the entry fee, and a hunting license could join the drive, regardless whether they were levelheaded, totally sober, or knew how to handle firearms. At the peak of the drive, when the circle was 100 yards or less across, it became apparent who was who. Some people became so overwhelmed with the excitement of killing they went into fits of puking or maniacal laughter. Others, in various stages of inebriation, shot inside the circle, so focused on a rabbit that they lost all track of other hunters. This raised outraged cries from across the diameter or on secants, "Shoot outside, goddammit, you almost hit me!"

People occasionally appeared to hit the same rabbit simultaneously, leading to squabbling over whose it was—as if it mattered, for the animals all went into a big pile for the same cause.

The rabbit drive covered only a tiny fraction of the area of the Valley, and its effect on the overall jackrabbit population was thus vanishingly close to zero. The amount of money raised for the sponsoring organization was likely offset by the risk of a lawsuit if someone were shot accidently—a risk that was, in contrast to the effect on the rabbit population, not vanishing close to zero. All considered, there seemed to be no good reason for the drive, except that it helped break the monotony of living in the Valley.

Chapter 8 – The Armory dojo

Is judo injurious to the female? Can the female frame take the punishment?

—E.K. Koiwai, M.D. in *Official AAU - JBBF Judo Handbook*, 1966

My family moved to Taos, NM for 6–8 weeks in the summer of 1964, and I missed this span of judo practices. Practices may've been interrupted for part of this period anyway, for when I returned to Alamosa in late July, SLV was in the process of moving to a new location, the Colorado National Guard Armory on the corner of Murphy Drive and First Street toward the west edge of town. The Armory was a cavernous, ugly, yellow-stucco building, and we had access to half of it.

We dismantled the frame for our mat from the Courier building and reassembled it in the Armory. We then hauled in sawdust by dump truck and shoveled it by hand into the frame. In further research on mat construction, the Judge'd learned that burying used automobile tires in the sawdust would improve the stability of the mat and give it more spring. We did this, but I don't remember whether we covered the whole floor inside the frame with tires or spaced them several feet apart.

After we'd completed the mat by stretching the canvas over the sawdust, we erected a chicken-wire barrier 10 feet tall to separate our dojo in the north half of the building from the south half, still occupied by the National Guard. We covered the barrier with bamboo screening to make it more attractive, and this is where we hung a new, 6-foot by 5-foot enlargement of our club insignia, reproduced in full color with felt cloth.

In our part of the building, the entrance on the north side opened onto a hallway, with an office off one side and a restroom and office off the other. We converted the offices to men's and women's changing rooms.

Bill Peterson started judo around this time. He was in the same year in school as Laurier, Kent, and I and remembers working on the Armory dojo during hot summer days, all of us drinking copious amounts of A&W root beer to stay hydrated. Bill later competed on our five-man team and eventually reached brown-belt rank.

On Saturday, 22 August 1964, SLV held a "housewarming" to inaugurate the new dojo. An eminent contingent traveled from Denver for the event, including Tooru Takamatsu (by then, 6th dan and 2nd Vice-President of the Judo Black Belt Federation) and his family; two of his coaches, Leroy Abe (2nd dan and 1964 Rocky Mountain AAU overall judo champion) and James Sakabe (3nd dan); a seven-member women's team (juniors to seniors); and several parents who transported participants.

The most significant event at the housewarming was Eddie's promotion to 2nd dan. **[Illustration, p. 156]** He deserved it, for under his training, SLV was gradually becoming noticed in Rocky Mountain judo. Takamatsu Sensei came through for Eddie, supporting him to the hilt.

In another event, Laurel Yasui and Jeannie Hall from Denver performed the Nage No Kata, which translates as "Forms of Throwing." Kata in general are a highly stylized mode of practice whereby both thrower and faller cooperate to perform a particular set of techniques with ideal form. In the Nage No Kata, 15 techniques, three each from the five categories of throws, are executed on both the right and left sides, with one person the designated thrower and the other the faller. Finally, there was a one-on-one match between the Denver and SLV women's teams, which Denver handily won with five wins, one loss, and one draw.

In the evening, Judge Myers hosted a swimming party at Splashland and a hamburger barbeque in his backyard for the Denver and SLV women's teams. Harry Sumida and his wife entertained Eddie and the visiting adults with a steak fry at their home south of Fort Garland.

The Armory dojo was a fine place, with bright overhead fluorescent lighting and abundant space around all four sides of the mat for spectator chairs. Unfortunately, the tire theory did not entirely hold up. With intensive use, the mat developed scattered, tire-shaped hollows, and just as in the Courier building, we had to periodically draw back the canvas and level the sawdust.

Classes in the Armory dojo were not segregated by age or sex. Kids and adults, men and women, practiced at the same time, with the high-school and college students trying not to land on the grade schoolers.

In 1954, a 19-year-old named Gina "Rusty" Kanokogi (née Glickman) began judo in Brooklyn, NY. Unusual for her time, she preferred randori rather than kata and was grudgingly allowed to practice with the men's classes. In 1959, she decided to compete in the YMCA Judo Championship in Utica, NY—which everyone understood was a men's shiai, because there were no official shiai for women back then. Women weren't yet specifically barred from men's tournaments, nor was there a "gender" box to check on tournament applications. It was simply unthinkable that women could or would engage in a fighting competition.

Rusty thought, screw that, and entered with the support of her male teammates. Nonetheless, knowing which way the wind would blow, she took the precautions of cutting her hair and taping her breasts flat to disguise herself. She won her team match against a male opponent, and her team won the competition. When it came time for the presentation of medals, however, the officials asked whether she was a woman—the scuttlebutt'd made its rounds. When she replied she was, they stripped her of her medal and demanded she leave the podium.

Denied shiai competition in the US, Rusty traveled to the Kodokan to train. Women practiced separately from men there, too, but being so much stronger than her female counterparts, she again broke the sex barrier and was allowed to train with men. After promotion to 2nd dan, she returned to the US and, in 1966, organized and directed a women's fighting competition, the New York Women's Invitational Shiai.

In 1963, the AAU and JBBF jointly published the first Official AAU Judo Handbook, which was updated annually in succeeding years. In a section entitled "Women's Competition, Senior (17 years and over)," the 1963 Handbook included the unambiguous statement "Competition for women will be conducted in kata only" and went on to specify how kata competitions were to be conducted and scored.

The 1963 Handbook also included a section on JBBF rank requirements, which specified the exact knowledge, skills, and accomplishments necessary for ranks from 6th kyu to 6th dan for both men and women. Here there was a little crack in the dike holding back women from shiai competition, for the women's requirements for 2nd-kyu rank and above stated, "SHIAI: Contest judo for women is not required *nor desirable* [my italics] but may be left to the option of the female judoka candidate at this level."

With this statement, the JBBF acknowledged that women chafed at being restricted to kata and wanted the chance to rip the guts out of their sisters in shiai—although this clearly departed from what the male leadership considered to be acceptable feminine behavior. Women could optionally fight matches if they could find tournaments in which to do so, but these wouldn't be sponsored by the AAU. The rank requirements clearly specified a subservient role for women at 1st-dan rank, noting that they "should serve as recorders, timers, and misc. administrative duties connected with a tournament."

The 1966 Official AAU-JBBF Official Judo Handbook continued the restriction of official women's competition to kata, with the further restriction from the other direction that "No men may participate in Kata Competition except as officials." Apparently some of the guys'd started to get a little swishy, and it was time to put a stop to that—or perhaps some of the men demanded reciprocity in order to protest the intrusion of women into shiai, which they may've considered their domain.

Interestingly, the 1966 Handbook included within "Section 16—Women's Judo" a one-page analysis entitled "Women in judo—a medical standpoint" by Dr. E.K. Koiwai, MD. After admitting that his "not being a member of the fairer sex makes it rather difficult for me to answer for them," and some further hemming and hawing, the Doctor concluded, "Watching the women develop from rank beginners to experienced judoka and comparing them with men, I find that the difference is slight, if any."

⤸

This was the state of affairs from 1962 to 1967, when the San Luis Valley Judo Club came into being and reached its apex. I believe Takamatsu Sensei in Denver saw early on the future of women's judo and during this period made a concerted effort to develop women's shiai competition in the Rocky Mountain region. He may've tasked Eddie with developing women's judo at SLV so the Denver women'd have another club to compete with.

In February 1963, the Denver School started a "women's and girls' class," with Dr. Yoshio Ito (2nd dan, soon to become 3rd dan) as chief instructor. It's unclear whether this was the first women's instruction at DSJ, or whether some women'd already begun in the men's classes but would now have their own class. The class had 18 students and met for 2 hours on Saturday afternoons. A group photo from a news article in February 1963 shows 17 women students, all white belts, along with three instructors, including Prof. Masao Ichinoe (8th dan) visiting from the Kodokan.

In November 1963, Dr. Ito took a group of 10 women judoka to Colorado State University in Fort Collins, as part of a daylong clinic that also included men, for a "demonstration of feminine judo techniques," as a news article stated—unfortunate wording, for women use the same techniques in judo as men. Perhaps the reporter meant the women performed the Nage No Kata, which men also learn for 1st-kyu rank.

Indeed, the only difference between men's and women's judo was that women's colored belts had a median white stripe running the length of the belt. This seemed to signify lower rank for women than for men— as though they always remained partly of kyu rank. I can see no other explanation, for certainly a different belt isn't needed to distinguish men from women. The convention has since been scrapped.

In July 1964, a month before SLV Judo moved into the Armory dojo, Jack Oliver (2nd dan) was involved in preparing the Denver women's competitors for an upcoming National Women's Tournament in Mason City, Iowa, 11–13 September. The relevant news account is unclear whether this was kata or shiai format, but I suspect the latter, since neither "AAU" nor "Olympic" was appended to the tournament name. Women's classes in Denver were now being held twice a week, Wednesday evenings in addition to Saturday afternoons. Denver undoubtedly viewed the seven-woman team match between Denver and SLV in August 1964 as further preparation for the upcoming Nationals.

In a list of September 1964 promotions following the Women's Nationals, two senior Denver women reached 3rd-kyu brown belt; six intermediates, 3rd-kyu purple belt; and one junior, 3rd-kyu green belt. So, they'd all gone to the Nationals as white belts. I don't know how well the Denver women fared, but it's safe to say that in men's national competition, a white belt would've been demolished in short order.

Women's judo started at SLV soon after Eddie arrived in Alamosa in 1963 and not long after it started in Denver. By August 1964, when we moved to the Armory dojo, we had a solid core of girls and women ranging in age from 7-year-old Toni Bowers to 16-year-old Sara Lucero, a high-school student from Antonito at the south end of the Valley who commuted a 57-mile round trip to practices in Alamosa.

Sara was our star woman judoka, a tough, dedicated competitor and fun to be around. A top student in high school, she planned to become a doctor. Interestingly, in the group photo following the Denver/Alamosa women's team matches in August 1964, Sara is the only woman with a colored belt. The only match SLV won was probably hers.

As mentioned, there was no separation of men's and women's classes at SLV. We all bowed in and warmed up together. During randori, women tended to pair with women, and men with men, but not exclusively so. Sara preferentially worked out with the men because she was so much stronger than any of the other women. She was a handful—no shrinking violet there—who would've made Rusty Kanokogi proud. By 1965, many of the junior and intermediate women at SLV'd reached colored-belt kyu ranks.

Sometime in 1966, SLV put on a small tournament in the Adams State College gymnasium. I forget what clubs attended or whether it was restricted to women, but at that shiai Sara twisted out of a throw, landed on her front, and broke a collarbone. That and a broken arm in a men's match in Denver were the only broken bones I remember in 5 years of competitive judo.

In the same tournament, my sister Kathy, who was 14 and ranked purple belt, threw her match rather than her opponent. She hadn't wanted to compete in the first place, because she'd recently gotten dental braces and these chewed up the inside of her mouth. For some reason, she ended up in the tournament at the last minute. Scared to death and worried about her mouth, as soon as her match with a Denver girl started, she whispered to her opponent, "I don't want to be here; just throw me, fast!" Her opponent obliged. Kathy left judo soon after in favor of 4H rodeo, though it's a mystery why she was more terrified of a judo match than galloping around barrels on a 1200-lb horse.

Largely through the efforts of women like Rusty Kanokogi and men like Tooru Takamatsu in the 1960s, the status of women in judo gradually changed from their being ornaments to being active participants. The first national women's shiai sponsored by the AAU under the same rules as for men took place in 1974. Fuller integration on a global scale took time. Whereas men's judo has been an Olympic event nearly continuously since 1964, women's judo lagged almost three decades behind, added to the Olympics in 1992.

Women now compete at the same levels as men in local, regional, national, and international events, including the Olympics. An exciting new judo competition added to the World Championships in 2017 and to the Olympics in 2020 (2021) is the Mixed Team Event, with teams composed of three men and three women, each member competing in a different gender/weight class against the corresponding member of the opposing team.

⤳

My sister related to me years later that some of the younger girls hated Sara Lucero and would sharpen their toenails so as to cut her shins and ankles when they pretended to attempt footsweeps. I was shocked to learn this.

"How could anyone not like Sara?" I asked.

Kathy said, "Well, they didn't like her because she was Hispanic."

I digress here to note that many of the Anglos in the Valley considered themselves superior to Hispanics–Latinos–Chicanos (the politically correct terminology has varied) and derogatorily called them "Mexicans," the one thing they assuredly were not. Up to 1913, this term was institutionalized; according to a contemporary newspaper account, the schools in Alamosa were segregated into a "Mexican school south of the tracks" and two "English speaking schools" in North Alamosa. Latino kids had to attend the "Mexican school," whether or not they spoke English and even if the other schools were closer to where they lived. In 1913, a forward-thinking district judge named Holbrook ruled that Latino students would be allowed to attend the school nearest them—in other words, he ruled for school desegregation.

The Anglo anti-"Mexican" prejudice nonetheless remained entrenched and, as one might expect, engendered resentment in the opposite direction. This amounted to a lot of resentment, because Latinos comprised fully one-third of the student body when I was in high school. Entering 9th grade, my sister, who's one of the few truly race-colorblind people I've ever known, shared a locker with a tough Latina named Shirley. During a softball game in gym class, they'd been on opposite teams, and Shirley'd continuously trash-talked Kathy's team. She kept it up when they got back to their locker.

Finally fed up, Kathy said, "I spit on people like you" and then spat on her. The "people like you" epithet referred to Shirley's trash-talking rather than her cultural roots, but Shirley might've taken it the wrong way. That aside, the spitting was a clear-cut casus belli.

Shirley swung at Kathy, who ducked but not enough and caught an elbow in the eye, later resulting in a brilliant shiner. Kathy then proceeded, as she describes it, to "slap the living shit out of her." After thus establishing the boundaries of social decorum, they continued sharing the locker and got along fine.

Through this single dustup, Kathy—unlike the pathetic outcome of my inaugural fight in the Alamosa school system—garnered such a reputation for extreme violence that she had no further fights in her high-school career. She was Churchill to my Chamberlain.

Aside from the Sara Lucero story, I never saw or learned of any racism in the judo club, which included African Americans, Japanese, Latinos, Native Americans, and various flavors of Anglos at one time or another. Most of us knew Eddie'd been thrown into a concentration camp by the largely Anglo US Government, yet here he was teaching us. To behave differently would've been a slap in the face to him.

Racism and its bastard sister nationalism do occur in judo but are rare and not tolerated. In a notorious incident in the 2016 Olympics in Rio de Janeiro, after Egyptian judoka Islam El Shehaby lost to the Israeli Ori Sasson, he refused to shake Sasson's offered hand and tried to leave the mat without bowing. The referee called him back to bow, which he did, but the crowd booed him as he departed. El Shehaby quit judo soon after.

In another incident, Algerian judoka Fethi Nourine withdrew from his scheduled competition in the 2020 (2021) Tokyo Olympics because he was on a course to face the Israeli Tohar Butbul, stating support for the Palestinian cause as his reason. As he'd done this sort of thing before, the IJF finally lost patience and suspended him and his coach for 10 years for breaching the Olympic Charter and Code of Ethics.

Chapter 9 – Small-town life

In the early stages of judo training, students, especially young people, sometimes feel tempted to try out their newly learned techniques on unsuspecting persons. Such behavior is irresponsible and highly dangerous. ... The only time one is justified in applying judo techniques outside the dojo is when in immediate physical danger.

—*Kodokan Judo* by Jigoro Kano

Sometime in fall 1963 after Eddie arrived in Alamosa, he began testing those of us he felt were ready for promotion to 4th kyu, the highest level of white belt. This was necessary so that when we started competing, we'd be eligible for promotion to 3rd kyu, the lowest colored-belt rank. I've already described the ranking system, but not how the ranks are determined. Several factors are involved: knowledge, competition, time-in-rank, and service to judo.

When you begin judo, you are automatically 6th kyu. All you have to do is show up and put on your new white belt.

For 5th kyu, you need to know the basics: how to fall, how to grip your opponent, how and when to bow, the basic natural and defensive postures, and the basics of getting your opponent off-balance, getting in position, and performing a throw. You also need to know a specified four throwing techniques and two pinning techniques. You can easily learn all this in a month or two.

For 4th kyu, you need to improve the throws you learned for 5th kyu and learn an additional four throwing and two pinning techniques.

For testing, Eddie took us onto the mat one by one while the others waited in the dressing room and asked us to demonstrate the required techniques. He used a faller other than himself so that he remained free to observe; each person who got tested stayed on as the faller for the next person.

For the 4th-kyu test, he'd name throws in Japanese and we'd do them. The test was anticlimactic. Of course we knew the basics, just by attending practices. Of course we knew the required eight throws—actually, many more than this—and four pins. The test seemed ludicrously easy, almost a sham, but it wasn't a sham. It made us realize formally how much we'd learned without being aware of it.

For 3rd kyu, the first colored-belt rank, you officially need to know the ranking system, colors of belts, and purposes of kata and randori—duh! You need to learn another four throws, two more pins, and two choking techniques. At this point, competition and time-in-rank come into play. If you know the required techniques, with continuous attendance but no competition, you're eligible for promotion to 3rd kyu after 9 months as 4th kyu. If you succeed in competition against your own or higher ranks, you can be promoted more quickly.

This gives the general idea how rank is determined in judo, and promotion criteria through the rest of the kyu ranks to about 3rd dan include a similarly stated component of specific knowledge. Advancement in the lower dan ranks can be based heavily on competition. Judoka competing frequently at the international level and placing in the World Championships or Olympics might reach as high as 5th or 6th dan largely through competition. Promotion after retirement from competition is based on time-in-rank and service to judo, including running a dojo, coaching, organizing and overseeing tournaments, functioning as judge or referee, or active involvement in the administration of a judo organization.

Eddie gave us no more formal tests after we reached 4th kyu, but we would've passed them easily. I'm sure we could execute most of the 40 throws in the Go Kyo No Waza by the time we'd been in judo a year and a half. The math is simple; at the rate of one new throw a week, it would've taken only 10 months to learn 40 throws. By the time we moved into the Armory building in August 1964, all of us remaining from Sammy Tahara's original group and some who'd started later had reached at least 3rd-kyu rank and wore a green, purple, or brown belt according to age.

Promotion above 4th kyu requires you begin to learn the Nage No Kata—the first three sets for 3rd and 2nd kyu, and all five sets for 1st kyu. After we moved to the Armory dojo, however, Eddie taught all of us ranked 3rd kyu and above the entire five sets, which we took turns practicing as thrower and faller.

For rank promotions, judo federations now use elaborate systems that assign competition points or fractions thereof to ippon and waza-ari wins in accredited local, regional, national, and international tournaments against opponents of higher, lower, or equal ranks. The more points you accumulate, the less time-in-rank you need before promotion. There were no personal computers in the 1960s, however, to keep track of such a mass of information within and across regions, and I certainly never saw Eddie writing anything down. On the other hand, I'm sure he had a rough idea how we stood on the basis of our placements in tournaments.

Eddie had full autonomy to promote any of us as he wished within the kyu ranks and used this authority judiciously. **[Illustration, p. 157]** He had little reason to inflate our ranks—it wasn't as though he'd get a pay raise if a lot of us advanced. In any case, Takamatsu Sensei was Chairman of the Board of Examiners of the Rocky Mountain Yudanshakai (yudanshakai = regional black-belt association), through which all promotions were registered, and he approved Eddie's promotions. In fact, Takamatsu himself promoted some of us after wins in Denver.

Promotions were not something most of us at SLV strove for. Quite the opposite, they were a mixed blessing. If you held colored-belt rank, you were open to humiliating losses to white belts. As a white belt, it was win-win; you felt great if you beat a colored belt but no humiliation if one beat you. The same logic held within the various colored-belt ranks.

↩

Late in 1964, my mother started the Valley Bookstore. I mention this because it was situated in an old house next door to Eddie's, both of them on the same lot across Main Street from the high school. This meant that if I didn't feel like walking home after school, I could simply cross the street, hang out in the bookstore until closing time, and ride home with my mother. Occasionally, when she had errands to run, she put me to work manning the cash register.

For me, the bookstore had two important consequences. Because my mother had to stay in Alamosa to run the store, from 1965 on, I didn't have to move to Taos, where my father worked in the summers, and miss 6–8 weeks of judo. In addition, I was often at the bookstore when Eddie came home from work and thus gradually got to know him outside the judo club. Sometimes he'd invite me in to talk while he cooked dinner and I waited to go home.

By 1964–65, my sophomore year, a number of high-school students were involved in judo. Because the novelty of the sport hadn't yet worn off, we thought it was cute to come up behind a fellow judoka as he was walking in the halls and tap one of his feet with a mild footsweep, just enough to cause him to stumble awkwardly. This got out of hand one day when a guy not in judo said something derogatory to Kent, who flattened him with a footsweep, knocking his wind out. This may not've been entirely intentional, for there's nothing easier than a footsweep on an untrained person. To avoid further incidents, we instituted a "no footsweeps in the halls" rule.

That year, my locker was on the lower tier in the corner of a hall cul-de-sac in front of Mrs. Lester's English class. One day, a junior named Tom was in the hall waiting for English class to start as I was rushing to my locker to get books for my next class somewhere else. Deciding it would be entertaining to make me be late for class, Tom crouched with his back to the wall, his legs bent at a right angle in front of him, blocking my locker.

The reptilian part of my burgeoning judo brain said to itself, "Wow, what an opportunity," and without thinking, I put a hand on his left shoulder, hooked his legs out from under him with my right leg, and dragged him onto his back, away from my locker. He ended up close to the open doorway of the English class.

Enraged with humiliation, Tom proceeded to pummel me aimlessly with his fists in an uncontrolled tantrum. I turned my back to him, so he didn't do any damage. When he stopped, I turned to face him. "If you ever do that again, I'll fucking kill you," he said.

I said, "If you ever get in front of my locker again, I'll throw you again," though it was hardly a throw. The class bell rang, and we left it at that. I figured I was in for further retribution.

Tom was close friends with Bill Anders, a tall, wiry, blond guy with black-frame glasses. Both were in the "tough guy" clique at school, guys you didn't mess with. This was the crowd who crossed to the other side of Main Street to smoke in full view of the Principal's office, knowing they were out of his jurisdiction. I didn't see much of Bill at school, but he was in the judo club, where he was friendly and worked hard. I liked him a lot.

The day after the locker incident—I'd told no one about it—Bill came up to me at school and said, grinning, "I heard you had a little run-in with Tom."

"Yeah, he tried to block me from my locker and I knocked his legs out from under him. He's going to want revenge," I said.

"Naw," said Bill, "I don't think he'll bother you anymore."

At a tournament in Denver during the 1965 season, Bill was doing well but twisted a knee in a match. He was sitting in the stands afterward, wrapping the knee, when Eddie came up to take a look. Eddie decided the sprain was bad enough that further injury might be permanent and pulled him from the competition. Bill burst into sobs of frustration and disappointment, for he was a fighter and wanted to keep going.

It was unforgettable, this tough guy crying because he couldn't go out and get the crap knocked out of him some more. At that moment, I lost all fear of the schoolyard, for I realized it held nothing as rough as fighting four or five judo matches in a day.

⌒

The Armory dojo was close to Adams State College, and we began to get an increasing number of college students, many of whom were active in competition and reached brown-belt rank.

Harold Hock, one of SLV's founding members, was still active. His goal was to enter West Point Military Academy, but he had to wait for a nomination from one of Colorado's US senators or congressmen. This took several years, and in the meantime he enrolled in classes at Adams State.

Another active member was Chuck Gutierrez. We had a connection, because his cousin Dolores Torres'd been my father's student 10 years before at Trinidad State Junior College. Dolores was from an old, prosperous ranching family in eastern Colorado and was gorgeous. The male college students in Trinidad'd tripped over their tongues trying to get her attention, and at 6 years old I'd also been in love with her and resented them as rivals.

Bob Anderson was an NCAA champion wrestler. Enormously powerful, with a physique like you see in Greek sculptures, he could've pinned any of us high schoolers whenever he chose, but he wanted to learn to throw. Because of his strength, he was formidable in randori even as a beginner, and through him we gained experience in dealing with much stronger opponents.

Artie Spano was a funny little Italian guy from New Jersey whose father ran a garbage truck across the river in New York. Once, after practice, we were talking about firearms, a topic that arose because one of Artie's friends'd been arrested in a bar in downtown Alamosa for having a concealed revolver. Artie was indignant.

"It's no big deal. No one from Joisey in his right mind goes to da City at night wit'out a piece on him."

When I asked what he intended to do after graduation from Adams State, Artic looked at me as though I were a half-wit. "Waddya think I'm gonna do? I can make 40 grand a year woikin' on da garbage truck. I ain't gonna do no better'n that wit' my college degree." I neglected to ask him why he was in college and specifically why in Alamosa.

Richard "Rich" Copenhagen was a big guy from the Bay Area in California who started judo in the Armory in fall 1964, soon after arriving for his first year at Adams State. He and another heavyweight named Mike started together and, after they'd learned to fall and knew a few throwing techniques, began to engage in randori.

"You and Kent Myers," he recollected, "really cleaned our clocks. We couldn't believe it. I was so impressed that smaller guys could throw us big guys easily and pretty much at will, I knew I had to continue with judo." Mike had a different reaction and quit judo.

Rich was remarkably good-natured, and he and Eddie became close friends. In the fall of 1965, Eddie rented him a spare bedroom in his house and they became housemates. Both of them hailing from California, they were kindred spirits; like Eddie, Rich came to love judo, and they both loved beer.

As a testament to the latter, Rich recounted how they stacked cardboard beer cases filled with empty bottles along the outer wall of the hallway running the length of their house, noting that "The beer cases pretty much held our house up." When Rich was getting ready to leave Alamosa upon graduation in 1968, Coors beer company was having a redemption campaign where it paid 1 cent each for bottles. Eddie and Rich turned in all their empties—accumulated through day-to-day drinking and parties during the 5 years Eddie (and for 3 years, Rich) had occupied the house— for a total of $156. This amounted to 15,600 beer bottles, which must've been some kind of record. **[Illustration, p. 164]**

⌒

Before our second full season of competition in 1965 **[Illustration, p. 158]**, Judge Myers took orders for custom-made black windbreakers to give us a team identity. These had our name sewn in yellow script above the SLV Judo patch on the left front and "ROCKY MTN." in a semicircle of big, yellow letters across the upper back. **[Illustration, p. 154]**

By this time, we were becoming experienced in competition. Each of us had his idiosyncratic taping ritual, reinforcing bad ankles or wrists. Before matches, we coated our sleeves and lapels liberally with unscented talcum powder to make them more difficult for our opponents to grip. While I can't find anything in the old rules stating this was illegal, it might've been, so we did it surreptitiously. We thought we were very clever, but the Denver guys probably did it too—after all, we'd learned it from Eddie.

A humorous incident happened that year at a tournament in Pueblo. One of our juniors was Craig Kelso, who viewed judo primarily as wrestling. He had a match in the 10-year-old division against a Denver opponent, Joey Takamatsu, who was much more experienced. Joey's father, Takamatsu Sensei, was referee.

During the match, Craig assumed a defensive posture, bent low and holding his arms stiff to prevent Joey from getting close. If Joey did manage to get past the arms, Craig's response was to drop face-first to the mat, hoping to entice Joey into wrestling. This overly defensive behavior was technically illegal, but Takamatsu Sensei might've hesitated to penalize or disqualify Craig for fear it'd look like favoritism.

It's extremely frustrating when an opponent stiff-arms you. Joey finally snapped, and when Craig dropped to the mat for the nth time, suddenly kicked him in the head. This was a major, unambiguous rule violation. Takamatsu Sensei unceremoniously yanked Joey back to the starting position, gave him a couple of swats on the butt, said "Shame on you," and awarded the match to Craig. I sympathized with Joey, for many were the times I'd felt like kicking a stiff-armer in the head.

Though I was in Alamosa the summer of 1965, I had an enforced absence from judo nonetheless. I developed a growth, like a big wart, on the middle toe of my left foot. Our family doctor decided it might be cancerous and said it should be removed, which he did himself. He didn't just remove the wart but amputated the whole distal phalange of the toe, performing the surgery in a hospital room. To my knowledge, he didn't ordinarily do much surgery, and during the procedure he seemed like a little boy pretending to be a surgeon.

I spent a night in the hospital and then recovered at home. The two following nights were the most painful I've ever experienced, yet all the damned doctor allowed me was aspirin. A pathologist returned negative test results, and I don't think the operation was necessary—the doctor could've just as well taken a biopsy and sent that off. I learned much later that he'd kept a secret mistress for decades, had bought her a house and furnished it, and so perhaps he needed the money. Whatever the case, I was on crutches and out of judo for 2–3 weeks. I used the time to plant and tend a small garden in the miserable, sandy soil behind our crackerbox house on 10th Street.

Later the same year, I had further foot problems. Since I had long legs and size-11 feet with long toes, I had an advantage in leg techniques and used them a lot. During randori one day, I attempted a footsweep and caught my right small toe in a fold of my opponent's pants. I heard a pop, looked down, and saw my toe bent out at a right angle from where it should've been. The sight of the injury was a lot worse than the pain of it. Eddie popped the toe back into place.

"It's probably just dislocated," he said, "but you better get it checked." He drove me the few blocks to the hospital ER for an X-ray. It was just dislocated.

After doing the same thing to a big toe several months later, I developed a fear of dislocations that inhibited practicing freely. The solution was to tape the large and small toes on each foot to the adjacent toes, and then wrap tape around the pad and toes of each foot. This taping ritual, which I came to perform before every practice and competition, had a downside— while it kept my toes from getting dislocated, the edges of the tape tended to curl up, exposing some adhesive and making my feet slightly sticky on the mat, thus slightly slowing footwork.

Eddie, in a fit of humor regarding my fondness for footsweeps and dislocating toes, brought black, red, orange, and yellow marking pens with indelible ink to practice one evening and drew long, ornate flames erupting from the SLV insignia and both upper lapels of my judo gi. "You're so smoking hot with your footsweeps," he said, "I thought you needed some flames." It was my grungy workout gi rather than the one I used for competition, so it didn't matter—and I liked the flames.

∽

Laurier and I spent a lot of time in summer 1965 wandering along the Rio Grande east of town. For a while, we went after big, brown river carp, some of them 3 feet long, like living logs. We first tried to use a bow and tethered arrow, but the line attached to the arrow usually tangled, and we missed anyway due to refraction. We then switched to long spears. The fish easily eluded us in deeper water, but occasionally we drove one into a shallow inlet where we could get at him. The obvious way to catch them would've been fishing poles, but in our view, the big carp deserved more of a fighting chance than that. The fish were elusive enough that they accounted for many hours of fruitless, muddy effort, and we didn't get more than two or three of them.

I wonder why we were so bent on killing them. There was no reason to, because we didn't eat them, although we'd heard some of the locals did. These were the common carp, *Cyprinus carpio*, a delicacy in Europe since Roman times, introduced to the US from Europe in the 1830s, and a close cousin to the Asian carp from which ornamental Japanese koi originated. As post hoc justification, common carp are now considered detrimental to native fishes and ecosystems, so we may've been performing a community service in removing them from the Rio Grande.

On one of our carp expeditions, we discovered a hobo camped in the woods along the railroad tracks. He didn't see us. Deciding to help him, we raided our parents' pantries for canned goods that wouldn't readily be missed and took the food to him on our next carp expedition. He was a shaggy, grimy, bearded, middle-aged guy who looked much the worse for wear in tattered clothing. This time, he spotted us as we approached his camp.

"Hey there," one of us said, "we don't mean any harm; we just brought you some food."

"I don't need your food," he shouted. "Just stay the hell away from me." He began pelting us with slag rocks from the track bed and chased us for 50 yards. The next time we returned to the river, he was gone.

⇁

After SLV Judo moved into the Armory building, we started holding teriyaki-and-rice dinners every few months. I forget whether these were benefits to raise money, or simply social events. All club members and their families were invited.

To make teriyaki, you marinate meat in a mixture of diluted soy sauce, mirin (a sweet rice wine), sake (another type of rice wine), and fresh-grated ginger and cook it by frying or broiling. You can use any meat, but teriyaki's best with beef strips or chicken thighs, legs, or wings. Eddie was a teriyaki master but couldn't get all the proper ingredients in Alamosa. Although sake was available, he had to substitute ginger ale for the mirin and grated ginger.

For these events, Eddie fired up a charcoal grill outside the entrance to the dojo and broiled chicken and beef he'd marinated at home. I believe he also cooked big pots of rice at home and brought those. No one else knew how to make Japanese rice, which is sticker than typical Western rice and cooked by steaming with just the right amount of water rather than by boiling. You can easily screw up Japanese rice if you don't know what you're doing. Other people brought salads, soft drinks, and paper plates and cups. No one got cutlery—if you were going to eat teriyaki and rice, you had to do it right. After the cooking was done, Eddie demonstrated how to use the disposable chopsticks he'd brought in bulk from Denver.

Takamatsu Sensei's qualification that Eddie could return to Denver if he didn't like Alamosa—supposing he actually said that—proved to be unnecessary, because Eddie was now at home in Alamosa. He was widely known and well liked. His coworkers at Adams State called him Kamikaze Eddie, because he drove the big, professional riding mowers at breakneck speed like he was in a lawnmower derby. He'd been pushing or driving lawn mowers since junior high school, and the speed kept him from getting bored.

Next to judo, Eddie's favorite activity was partying. His sister Carolyn described him after he'd had a few beers as "funny and a little macho," and that fits perfectly. He'd deliver one-liners like, "Confucius say: woman who fly upside down have hairy crack-up" in a fake Chinese accent. He'd gossip, tell judo stories, and revile the Johnson administration's escalation of the Vietnam War, sometimes seguing into a karate kata.

An expression he used when he was feeling mellow was "Right on, cachetón," with "on" and "-tón" rhyming with "own." "Right on" was a familiar phrase from the '60s and pot-befuzzed '70s, but "cachetón" was pure Valley Spanish, in this context meaning something like "buddy."

Another funny, quirky expression he used to indicate mock surprise was "unberievabul"—"unbelievable" pronounced with a fake Japanese accent that converted the first "l" to an "r" and the second "l" to something between "l" and "r." Eddie had no Japanese accent, and with this he mocked his Japaneseness to amusing effect.

Eddie sometimes went out drinking with college students from the judo club—on Saturday nights, you might find him at Beef's or the Purple Pig—and knew a lot of people in the bars. The bars in Alamosa were rough; when people got loaded, their inhibitions got unloaded. Latinos'd fight with Anglos, college students with farmers, or any combination thereof. Everyone had a good ol' time.

It was curious that Eddie, only 5 feet 3 inches tall, somehow earned a reputation such that no one screwed with him. Once one of the college students came to judo practice on a Monday evening marveling at what he'd seen that weekend. Eddie'd been standing at the crowded bar in Beef's nursing a beer, when a big, tattooed pachuco (Latino gang member; young tough) backed into him. The guy turned around full of automatic venom, starting to say something like, "Why don't you watch where the fuck you're going?" When he saw it was Eddie, he held up his open hands and said instead, "Sorry, I didn't notice you there. I didn't mean to bump you," and edged away as fast as he could.

So, where did an inscrutable shrimp like Eddie get a reputation? Once—and this was later, when we high schoolers partied at his house on weekends—a half-lubricated Laurier Couture grabbed him in a judo stance, for what purpose remains obscure, and before you could say Jack Robinson, Eddie threw him with seoi-nage into the big heating stove in the living room, knocking down the stack. Luckily, it was summer. Taken aback, Laurier said, "Sensei, why'd you do that?" Eddie said, a little miffed, "Hey, you're the one who grabbed me."

I imagine Eddie's reputation downtown originated in the same way. A college student from the judo club, drunk in one of the bars, might've playfully grabbed him in a judo stance, whereupon Eddie threw him spectacularly and then finished up with some masterful karate blows (stopping short, of course). It would've been intimidating to anyone else in the bar. Onlookers'd be thinking, "Man, I wouldn't want to tangle with that mean little sonofabitch." Even big guys'd shy away from him for fear of getting their ass kicked by a shrimp.

Eddie really was inscrutable. He was impish and talkative around people he knew but clammed up around people he didn't. If a stranger tried to make conversation, he'd engage enough to be polite but offer nothing more. When he was annoyed or didn't want to talk, he had an unconscious quirk of slightly shaking his head—so slight it seemed almost a nervous tic—as though he was shaking off a bothersome insect. I never saw anyone insult him, but if they had, I doubt he'd have reciprocated. He'd just have looked inscrutable. I believe this reticence unnerved aggressive people, made them wonder what he had up his sleeve they didn't know about.

Ultimately, I suspect anyone who seriously tried to pick a fight with Eddie in a bar would've instantly had half the clientele pounding on him, for Eddie had a lot of friends. If push came to shove, though, I'm sure he could handle himself.

84

This picture might not tally with some people's image of a judo sensei. The fact is, judo teachers come from all walks of life. Takamatsu Sensei owned a potato-distribution company and loved to gamble. Other of the high-ranking Denver instructors were doctors or dentists. Various of the Japanese judoka at the Denver School were truck farmers or gardeners. Leroy Abe loaded and delivered sacks of potatoes all day for Takamatsu. One strong Denver black belt did a year or two in jail for burglary, caught after dropping his wallet in the garage of a home he'd just robbed. Everyone welcomed him back when he returned to judo, figuring he'd done his time. The only criticism I heard was people wondering how he could've been so careless as to drop his wallet.

Off the mat, Eddie was a workingman, with a workingman's proclivities. On the mat, he was a dedicated, skilled teacher, his demeanor serious but not austere. He was very good with the juniors and preferentially engaged them in randori, obviously enjoying it. He had the best of worlds. He could roughhouse with his kids every evening but then send them home for someone else to deal with the tedious task of putting them to bed. Sometimes when they started fooling around, he'd growl at them, "Hey, you guys, knock it off!" and they knocked it off. When he turned away, he had a twinkle in his eye, and you could see he was trying hard not to grin.

Eddie never demanded respect. He earned it.

〜

In 1965, Alamosa built a new high school on Victoria Street at the western fringe of town, several blocks from the Armory dojo. The new school wasn't large enough for four classes of students, and so starting in the fall of 1965, 10th through 12th grades moved from the old high school on Main into the new building, leaving 9th grade in the old. Kent, Laurier, and I were entering 11th grade and thus finished out our last 2 years in the new school. A single-story edifice, it was less solidly built than the old school but more pleasant. Unlike the old, it had a cafeteria.

In 1965, SLV Judo had an exhibition match with a team from the town of Cortez in the southwestern corner of Colorado, held in the gymnasium of the new high school. Carl Myers recalls that "their team were all scrappy Ute kids who were wrestlers in judo gis." This reminds me that Alamosa wasn't the only small Colorado town with a judo club in the 1960s. Craig in northwestern Colorado had an active club that we visited twice for tournaments. Cortez and Alamosa were about the same size, whereas Craig was smaller.

Coincidentally with the new high school, in the fall of 1965, my family moved from the crackerbox house on 10th Street that we'd occupied for roughly 3 years into another rental near the intersection of State and 20th streets, over a mile south of Main on the way to the airport. This was an older, larger, more solidly built home with a fenced lawn in front, a large shop building adjacent that we used for storage, and a sizeable, weed-covered backyard. The spring after we moved in, a wind storm whipping across the Valley piled up sand three feet deep against the front fence and deposited a foot of it over the whole lawn. It was a big job to shovel it out.

Although I was now isolated from my friends in the old neighborhood, the new place had the advantage of being more rural. The only dwellings nearby were a trailer next door inhabited by a young man and his pregnant wife, and on the far side of that, a small homestead occupied by a school-teacher who I'll call Mr. Hertz, his wife, and two small daughters. The two families were related, the young man next door being Mr. Hertz's nephew. Otherwise, the countryside all around was chico brush. Our neighbors, however, proved to be on the gothic side of normal.

We had two black Labrador retrievers that my father used for duck hunting and a golden retriever named Rusty, who never did warm to the concept of retrieving but had a penchant for wandering. To confine the dogs during the day when no one was home, my father built a big frame-and-chicken-wire run in the backyard. Early mornings and evenings, we let the dogs roam freely, figuring they'd stay close when we were home.

A month or two after we moved to the place, Rusty showed up from an early-morning wander with a gaping gunshot wound in his gut and died on the doorstep. "Well, shit," said my father, "he must've gotten into someone's sheep—I guess we can't really blame them for shooting him. We have to be more careful."

To replace Rusty, we visited the pound and found a big golden Lab named Bob. Like Rusty, Bob didn't have much use for ducks but loved to chase rabbits. He was great for walks in the chico and soon became my favorite dog.

We were more careful for a time but got lax again keeping track of the dogs. Early one Saturday morning, we heard a not-too-distant shotgun blast, and Bob hobbled home soon after with his one of his shoulders blown away. We got him alive to the vet, but he died on the operating table. This time, we we'd heard the blast, which meant the shooting was close by.

Heartbroken and angry, I decided to check the neighborhood to see who might've done it. No one was out and about, but the Hertzes had rabbit pens in their yard, and alongside one of the pens I found a shotgun trap. This was a fixed shotgun with a trip string running ingeniously from the trigger back through a pulley and forward to a point next to the pen, where it was baited with a piece of meat. Anything tugging on the bait would trigger a shot. It was a chilling thing.

It happened that my Denver relatives were passing through town that day. In the evening, my father and Uncle George, reinforced with whiskey, decided something had to be done about the shotgun trap. They both strapped on holstered pistols—a classic recipe for disaster—and walked over to the Hertzes' place to have a talk. I didn't accompany them and don't know what was said, but no one got shot.

The following Monday, my parents called the County Sheriff to report the shotgun trap, as these were illegal—imagine Mr. Hertz's young daughters wandering out to see the pretty rabbits. Mr. Hertz was eventually convicted for that offense and cruelty to animals but went on teaching school.

The young couple in the trailer between us and the Hertzes seemed nice, said "hello" and all that, but one afternoon a year or two after the dog incidents, the guy came to our front door and asked to use our telephone. My sister, 14 or 15 years old and home alone after school, invited him in. The phone happened to ring just then and she answered it. Speaking to a friend, she turned back to signal the guy to wait a minute and saw that he'd dropped his pants and was masturbating. My sister told the friend not to hang up and screamed at the guy to leave the house, which he did.

When my father got home and learned of the incident, he called our landlord, who was also the young guy's landlord. By the following afternoon, the young couple'd been evicted and were gone. We all felt sorry for the guy's wife.

Such was our new neighborhood on south State Street.

Chapter 10 – Almost champions

Let us say that you have mastered a certain technique and are meeting an opponent. If you depend only on your favorite technique, the time will surely come when it will not work and you will find it difficult to win. This is because your opponent has thoroughly studied your technique as well as the flow of your matches and has devised countermeasures to neutralize you.

—Isao Inokuma in *Best Judo* by Isao Inokuma and Nobuyuki Sato

By the fall of 1965, we'd been training and competing hard for two seasons. While the relative beginners were undergoing the same initial string of defeats we'd endured, those of us who'd been in the club for 3 years were placing in tournaments more often than not. The astonishing thing was that we'd nearly caught up with guys in Denver who'd been in judo 7 or 8 years, who'd already been colored belts and placing in competition when we started. We didn't always beat them, not by a long shot, but we now had a fighting chance.

By the competition season of 1965–66, an intense rivalry'd developed between the SLV Judo Club and the Denver School. This came to a head in the Five-Man Team Championships in Denver in December 1965. SLV had a team in the Intermediate Division composed (in the order of matches) of Bill Peterson, Carl Myers, Laurier Couture, me, and Kent Myers. It was a big tournament, with 175 contestants from eight clubs making up 35 teams.

The format was "straight team competition," in which teams have equal numbers of players. The order of contestants on a team is fixed, so that each contestant competes with his opposite number in the lineup. The winning team is decided not by the absolute number of matches won, but by total points—10 points for an ippon win, 7 for a waza-ari win, and 5 for a win by judges' decision. By this system, a team can win three of five matches—for example, one by waza-ari and two by judges' decisions (a total of 17 points)—but still lose if the other team wins two matches by ippon (20 points).

Kent was our anchor man. After the first four matches, we were close to Denver in points, and his match would decide the outcome. The Denver School had bleachers along one side of the dojo large enough to hold 500 spectators, and they were full—mostly of Denver fans who were indignant that SLV might be about to beat them for 1st place. A lot of people knew and liked Eddie, but this was beyond the pale. They wished him success, but goddamn it, not *that* much success. While friends, families, and judo enthusiasts of all ages had turned out to watch, there seemed to be a preponderance of little old Japanese ladies who screamed and shook fists, tournament schedules, and canes during matches. They were out for blood. Our blood.

The reason it looked like SLV might win was that Kent was stronger, heavier, and higher in rank than his opponent, Steve Nakamura. When the match started, Kent engaged with an air of impatience, almost arrogance, as though it were a foregone conclusion he was going to win, and he couldn't wait to get it over with. This was vintage Kent. About a minute into the match, however, Steve caught him with a spectacular okuriashi-harai (double footsweep). Kent flew 3 feet high and came down hard. Of course it was an ippon.

Interestingly, Kent's brain simply could not process that it'd just lost. He started to continue the match, and the referee had to stop him. Hell, none of our brains could process it. In any case, the team match was over and Denver'd won. Amidst the roar of the little old ladies going apeshit in the crowd, Kent disappeared into the locker room, where we could hear him punching lockers.

Later I was able to piece together what'd happened. Before our team final started, I'd glanced over to the Denver warm-up area and noticed Leroy Abe talking animatedly with Steve Nakamura, and then Steve doing uchikomi with him, practicing some sort of counter. This was nothing out of the ordinary and I forgot about it, until it made sense later. What'd happened was that Leroy'd keenly observed our previous matches and noticed that when Kent hopped out from a failed attempt at seoi-otoshi, his favorite throw, both his feet left the ground for a split second. Leroy'd passed this tidbit on to Steve and had him practice the appropriate counter.

This was a good lesson—that one should never be arrogant going into a match, and as Sammy'd told us more than 3 years before, judo is as much a mental discipline as a physical one. To be successful, it behooves one to observe and think.

We were disappointed for Eddie's and our own sakes that we hadn't placed 1st, but we did split the difference—we'd beaten another Denver team for 2nd. That we'd gotten so close to 1st and scared the crap out of the little old ladies bolstered the Denver crowd's esteem for Eddie as much as if we'd won.

As the result of a 1st place in the 1966 Rank Championships in Denver, Kent Myers was promoted to 1st dan at age 16. He was the first black belt to emerge entirely from training at SLV.

↬

The same year, also at 16, I fought the match I remain most proud of. At a senior tournament in Denver, I came up against Joe Miley, who'd placed 3rd in the 140 lb division 4 years before at the 1962 National AAU Judo Championships in Chicago, half a year before I started judo. Ranked 2nd dan in 1962, he'd been a national-caliber competitor for years. Everyone, including me, expected Joe to make short work of me.

With this as a foregone conclusion, I determined to make the best of it. Eventually he scored a waza-ari with a throw, but I managed to hold him off for the rest of the 6-minute match. An explanation for this outcome was that he'd been out of judo for a couple of years and was out of condition.

After the match, I was talking to Eddie when Joe came up and said, "Wow, Eddie, your guys are tough!" It was a compliment to both of us.

↬

During the summer of 1966, two of us from SLV spent 6 weeks training at the Denver School, from mid-June to early August. I don't remember how this came about, whether it was Eddie's idea or due to an invitation from Takamatsu Sensei. A guy named Larry Schnider and I happened to be the two who went, largely because everyone else had other plans that summer. Larry was a high-school wrestler who used judo for training in the off season.

We slept on the tatami at night, prepared our meals in the Denver School's kitchen, and bathed in the shower room. Someone'd arranged jobs for us with a family of gardeners. I worked for a short, feisty little guy named Tom Taniguchi, and Larry worked for his son-in-law, Mr. Sakai. Mr. Taniguchi and his wife seemed to be issei but'd been in the US for decades. In his 50s, Mr. Taniguchi spoke little English, whereas his wife was moderately fluent. Their son Norio held 1st dan rank in judo. In his 20s and born in the US, he worked at Stapleton Airport preparing in-flight meals for Pan Am.

Taniguchi and Sakai were custom gardeners and had contracts in the summer months to care for the lawns and gardens of upper-class homes, most of them in and around the Belcaro district of South Denver. It was an affluent area, with curvy streets and expensive, widely spaced dwellings on large, manicured lots separated by wooden or stone fences. The homes came in styles ranging from Frank Lloyd Wright modern to faux European villa. It was a niche guys like Mr. Taniguchi virtually had a lock on; these homes were status symbols, and so was having a Japanese gardener.

Mr. Taniguchi's crew consisted of him, his wife, me, and one of two winos, the other being on Mr. Sakai's crew. The winos were either homeless or lived in flophouses in the vicinity of Larimer St. On any given day, either or both of them might not show up, which meant more work for the rest of us. On the other crew, Mrs. Sakai was not always present, as she sometimes had to stay home to care for the Sakais' young kids. The two crews occasionally worked together on large jobs but always separately on smaller ones.

Our bosses picked us up at the Denver School at 6 AM each morning, Monday through Saturday, though Saturdays we worked only half a day. Each of them drove a pickup truck and towed a flatbed trailer that carried the mowing machines, trimmers, blowers, and hand tools. The hired help rode in the back of the pickup. I enjoyed those rides through the clear, cool, early-morning Denver air before there was a lot of other traffic.

Mr. Taniguchi tended five to seven yards a day, returning weekly to each customer. Five yards may not seem like much, but some of them were extensive, with lawns bordered by ornamental gardens of flowers, shrubs, and small decorative trees.

On our crew, the wino and I were the grass cutters. We used Toro brand, gas-powered, self-propelled mowers that had four or five curved blades arranged in a horizontal, cylindrical assembly in front (like the old push mowers almost everyone used on their own lawns in those days), with a canvas grass catcher behind. These are called reel-type mowers as opposed to rotary mowers, which have a horizontal blade underneath (for some purpose, we had one of those, too).

It doesn't take much experience to cut grass, which is why the winos, Larry, and I were able to do it. The main thing is to start with a straight pass along one edge and then continue with parallel passes as you work your way up and back the length of the lawn, overlapping your cuts just enough so as not to leave strips uncut. Periodically as the grass catchers filled, we removed them and dumped the cuttings onto a large canvas tarp laid out in the yard. When the tarp filled, we folded it up and carried it to Mr. Sakai's truck, which we used to transport the cuttings.

While the wino and I worked on a lawn, Mr. Taniguchi and his wife tended garden beds—pulled weeds, broke up the soil with hand tillers, trimmed shrubs and trees, and spread mulch and fertilizer as necessary. After a lawn was cut, Mr. Taniguchi himself trimmed it along garden beds by hand, edged it along sidewalks using a gas-powered machine, and finally cleaned sidewalks and garden paths with a power blower.

Many of the lawns had underground sprinkler systems, with some of the sprinkler heads hidden in long grass. If you hit one, it put nicks in the mower blades that then left stripes down the cut lawn. The stripes were so faint that possibly the customers wouldn't notice them, but they offended Mr. Taniguchi's professionalism.

I had a penchant for hitting sprinkler heads. After the first one, Mr. Taniguchi routinely walked me around each lawn before I started cutting and showed me where the heads were. Once I started, however, I'd get hot and bored, my attention would wander, and bam! I'd hit another one. Mr. Taniguchi berated me in broken English.

"Baka!" (= fool) he'd say. "Fix blade, twen'-five dollah. You pay!"

After a while, he started calling me "Baka" as a nickname. I might not've hit the sprinkler heads if he'd marked them with red flags, but he didn't think to do this and it wasn't my position to suggest it. As it was, I only hit four or five in six weeks, but still, it cost him time and money. I was pretty inept; even the winos managed to avoid sprinkler heads. Probably the only reason Mr. Taniguchi didn't fire me was he could count on me showing up for work.

What struck me about the affluent neighborhoods we worked was that we scarcely saw a living soul—not through windows in the customers' homes, the yards we serviced, or anywhere on the streets or sidewalks. It was like being in a ghost town. This was good, because if we had to take a leak, we could do it in the shrubbery. These weren't the sort of clients where you rapped on the door and asked to use the bathroom.

92

We knocked off around 5 PM, and our bosses dropped Larry and me back at the Denver School. We barely had time for a quick dinner, usually a sandwich or warmed-up can of chili, before practice started at 7 PM. I don't remember much about the practices except that they were similar to those at SLV. A couple nights each week, one of the instructors'd explain techniques and we'd practice them. Other nights, we just did uchikomi, mat work, and randori. A big difference from SLV was that there were a lot more people of higher ranks to practice with.

Two black belts, Leroy Abe and Jack Oliver, also resided at the Denver School that summer and slept on the tatami. I don't know what Leroy's situation was—perhaps he was a live-in caretaker, better than a guard dog. Jack'd come up through the ranks at the Denver School and was on summer vacation from Colorado State University.

We all shared the kitchen, which was a mess. It was dirty when Larry and I arrived and went downhill from there. Neither of us did dishes but simply rinsed out what we needed for a meal and put the dirty dishes back in the sink. The kitchen reeked of rancid food, and cockroaches were rampant. Someone, probably Leroy, put up a sign, "Clean up—Your mother doesn't live here," but it didn't do any good. Leroy finally spent half a day cleaning the kitchen himself, which shamed us into better habits.

Jack Oliver was a puzzle. He claimed to know Japanese and sometimes before tournaments served as an usher to guide little old Japanese ladies into the bleachers so they could raise hell. The young Japanese judoka scoffed at him.

One of them said, "Jack knows about as much Japanese as my dog."

Some Sundays, Jack'd kneel in the seiza position on a cushion on the kitchen floor (ugh), wearing his judo gi, and practice shuji (Japanese brush calligraphy) on a big sheet of paper. I thought it was impressive, though it seemed the only characters he could write were those for "judo." I doubt it won much favor from the young Japanese judoka, who disdained him for engaging in Japanese culture while they were busy rejecting as much of it as they could.

A few times a week, after the formal practice, Jack singled me out for "special practice," though I was bone-tired from work and the evening's workout. We'd bow and start mat work, which consisted of him pinning me, removing my belt, and tying me up with it. He outweighed me by 40 pounds and ranked 2nd dan, so he could keep me completely under control as he did this. When I was immobilized, he'd walk away, leaving me trussed on the mat.

Jack claimed this was an ancient art that was somehow part of judo, and that he was doing me a favor by exposing me to it. Sometimes after I'd escaped from the belt, he did it a second time. When I tried to beg out initially or quit while it was underway, he pulled rank and informed me that one never asked a sensei to quit. I should've just refused to work out with him—what could he do?

Jack didn't try this nonsense on Larry Schnider, who was heavier and stronger than I and, being a wrestler, would've given him a hard time. I came to dislike Jack for these episodes and to view him as a bully. He'd managed to similarly alienate some of the other young judoka at the Denver School, so we finally devised a petty way to revenge ourselves. One of us bought a can of itching powder at a gag store, and every evening I sprinkled it liberally into Jack's bedding. Unfortunately, he never showed any signs it bothered him.

Prof. Masao Ichinoe, the 8th dan from Japan, attended practices at the Denver School for a week that summer, and I had several opportunities to do randori with him. He appeared to be somewhere in his 50s or 60s, though he might've been older. Before I engaged with the Professor, my friend Perry Yamashita took me aside and warned that I should not go full force with him nor strenuously attempt to throw him, even had I been able to. It would've been a bad breach of etiquette, as the Professor was long past his competitive years.

Perry cited an incident the previous year, when a young brown belt, after being similarly cautioned, had gone full-force with Ichinoe Sensei.

"To teach that guy a lesson afterwards," Perry said, "George Tagawa got him in randori and four-cornered him for 5 or 10 minutes."

George was a strong 1st dan and a good friend of Eddy. "Four-cornering" someone means to throw him in each corner of the mat, one after the other, around as many times as you feel he needs. Obviously you have to be a lot more skilled than your opponent to do this. The brown belt got the message—that the people he practiced with in randori often didn't go full force against him either.

It was an experience getting thrown by Ichinoe Sensei. He was so smooth and fast I sometimes didn't know what throw he'd just used.

⤶

During the 6 weeks at the Denver School, Larry and I were engaged in physical activity 12 hours a day. Often we didn't get to bed until after midnight and rose at 5 AM to prepare for work. After a week of this, I was severely sleep deprived and came to absolutely loathe the sound of the alarm clock in the morning, a visceral reaction akin to PTSD that lasted for years afterward.

My time in Denver was the first lengthy period I'd spent away from home, and Sundays I'd wander around the still moderately thriving Japantown district bordering on what came to be called Sakura Square at 19th and Larimer Streets, two blocks from the Denver School. A lot of small Japanese businesses remained—restaurants, cafes, grocery stores, barbershops, mercantile stores—but the district was in slow decline. Larimer street was a skid row, with seedy bars, porn parlors, whorehouses, flophouses, and greasy spoons. This district has since undergone urban renewal to become LoDo, Lower Downtown, and is now billed to have an active night life. There was an active night life back then, too, but a different kind of night life.

On the tawdry streets of Denver that summer, I experienced intense homesickness for the first and last time. It was loneliness, a feeling I didn't belong, a longing for the nest. The homesickness was good, for when I left Alamosa the following year to attend college, I'd gotten it out of my system.

I wasn't entirely alone, either. One Sunday, Takamatsu Sensei took Larry, me, and some other judoka to Elitch's amusement park, where he parked himself at a pachinko machine and left the rest of us to our own devices. Another Sunday, I visited my cousins in South Denver. Eddie drove up from Alamosa one or two weekends, ostensibly to check on Larry and me but mostly to visit friends, eat Japanese food, and take in the night scene on Larimer. By this time, he was driving a 1960s-model white Ford pickup; he'd parked his old, white station wagon next to his house to provide shade for the weeds.

When I started working for Mr. Taniguchi, he mentioned nothing about money. I didn't know what my hourly wage was and didn't receive a dime from him the whole 6 weeks I worked. In fact, I began to wonder whether I was getting paid at all. On my last day of work in August, however, he gave me a detailed list of the hours I'd put in and, to my great surprise, $700 in cash. This averaged to double the minimum wage—even more, if he'd made good on his threat to deduct the cost of sharpening the mower blades I'd dinged. It was very generous.

During my stay in Denver, I'd made friends with a brown belt about my age surnamed Eason. I've forgotten his first name—call him Danny. He, a brother, and a sister were in judo. They belonged to one of those families where all the offspring bear a striking resemblance to one of their parents; in this case, they all looked like miniature versions of their dad. My last week, Danny invited me to have dinner with him at a Mexican restaurant.

"What for?" I asked.

"You know, just have dinner, shoot the bull, enjoy each other's company," he said.

I mention this because it made me realize how different the cultures were between country mice and town mice, to borrow from Aesop. I literally didn't understand why he wanted to have dinner together. This just wasn't something my friends and I did. In Alamosa, we ate dinner at home, and when we met our friends, it was for some activity, like judo, work, or outdoor diversions. Outdoor diversions mostly involved riding, climbing, or killing something (e.g., horses, mountains, ducks), opportunities for which were limited in Denver.

The cultural differences extended to other spheres. My Denver aunt and cousins, for example, often talked about "The Mall" in the context of intending to go there or having just returned from there. I'd never been to a mall, didn't know what one was, nor even particularly cared. Another three decades would pass before I finally set foot in one.

The last thing I did at the Denver School was visit Takamatsu Sensei in his office and give him $75 for six weeks' housing and tuition. Like Mr. Taniguchi, he'd said nothing about money, but I figured the School could use it.

My mother and sister drove from Alamosa to pick me up. The evening before we left, Mrs. Taniguchi phoned my relatives' place, asking where I was staying. Mr. Taniguchi stopped by early the next morning and presented my mother with a case of fresh grapes he'd picked up at a wholesale market. "Baka," he said to me, "you wan' nex'-summa job, you come."

After I returned from the Denver School, Laurier Couture, Larry Schnider, Larry's friend Dean, and I worked for several weeks for a Valley contractor named Vic Crow, who was Bob Bowers's brother-in-law. Vic's specialty was digging ponds and reservoirs, and he hired us to riprap the banks of a reservoir with baseball- to football-sized stones. This involved first driving a dump truck to one of the big clearcut areas at the base of Mt. Blanca and loading stones by hand. After dumping them next to the reservoir, we placed them by hand a layer or two deep around inflow and outflow areas. It had to look nice. This was almost unbearably hot work in the high-desert sun of August, but it was good conditioning.

Dean was an obnoxious football jock. Once when we were on our way to work in Larry's car, with Dean riding shotgun and Laurier and I in the back, I made a remark about the Vietnam war that Dean took exception to. He said something like, "That's not right at all, and if you don't shut up, I'll kick your ass." It was unnecessary, mindless bullying. I thought, "How stupid is this guy? I'm behind him in a moving car; I could easily take off my belt, loop it around his neck, and choke him unconscious." But I let it slide. I felt sorry for him, for stupidity is an incurable condition.

Our boss, Vic Crow, was a character. Around 40 years old, about my height but stockier, he had the sandy complexion of a Midwesterner. At the onset of WWII, he'd joined other young vigilantes in the occasional vandalism of Japanese farms in the Valley. It was perhaps to make amends for this that he hired some of us from the judo club for summer work.

Vic was a self-styled philanthropist. He and his family lived near Mosca in a large, old, two-story farmhouse surrounded by outbuildings. As a lucrative sideline to his contracting business, he took on troubled young men from State juvenile detention facilities, housed them with his family, and attempted to set them on the right path through clean living and hard work. Sometimes he was successful but sometimes not. In an incident that forced him to rethink the whole wisdom of foster care, one of his wards herded ten or twenty of Vic's sheep into an outbuilding and slaughtered them with an axe.

After we finished the riprapping job, Vic kept Larry and me on for a short time to introduce us to heavy-equipment operation. I could see no other reason for this than his wanting to give us some experience. He had a full crew of seasoned construction men who'd worked with him for years, and he certainly didn't need beginners. He assigned Larry to run a road grader for a few days, removing brush and weeds from along barbwire fences.

Vic had me driving a dump truck most of the time, but one afternoon he put me on a sheepsfoot roller—a massive, tractor-like machine with a heavy steel drum in front. The drum was covered with staggered, blunt teeth that tamped down the earth as it rolled along. The roller was being used to compact the surface of a large, square, newly dug reservoir 20 or 30 feet deep. I compacted the bottom and then drove up a construction ramp to work around the periphery. On these level surfaces, it was like driving a slow car.

After I'd mastered driving on the level, Vic directed me to start on the steep banks. Not knowing how to do it, I headed at an angle down one side. As soon as I started, I heard a worker shout, "No, Vic!" The rest of his crew, scattered around the site, stopped what they were doing and watched. They knew it was a toss-up whether I was going to topple the big machine, and I felt the same.

After a nervous trip to the bottom, I parked the roller and got out. I forget how it ended with Vic, but that was the last I worked for him. Maybe it was a test and I'd failed it. That was okay. Vic basically had a good heart but sometimes not such good sense.

↶

Sometime in autumn 1966, Laurier Couture and I climbed Mt. Blanca. We borrowed Bob Bowers's old jeep and drove it up the rough, one-lane dirt road to Lake Como (unimaginatively named by a displaced Italian, no doubt). We camped by the lake and spent the afternoon trying to fish. The next day, we climbed from the lake to the summit. At 11,765 feet, the lake is only a mile and a half west-southwest of Blanca Peak but half a mile lower in elevation. Although the elevation presented no particular problem—we were acclimated to year-around living at 7600 feet—the steep final stretch was grueling.

The view from the top was worth the climb. Just as you can see Mt. Blanca from anywhere in the Valley, so you can see the whole, magnificent expanse of the Valley from the peak. When you're in the Valley, it just seems flat, but from Mt. Blanca you can see that it is, in fact, a high desert basin with slightly sloping sides—a vast, shallow bowl seemingly extending off into infinity. It is an unforgettable view.

↶

In rural America, deer hunting is a common rite of passage for teenaged boys. I had a .30-30 Model 94 Winchester lever-action rifle and the strong urge to kill something with it, a condition known as "buck fever." The opportunity arose in September, when Bob Bowers, understanding my affliction, offered to take me deer hunting in Crestone, a former mining town north of the Sand Dunes. The Bowers family owned an old home on the outskirts of town they used as a vacation getaway. Actually, Crestone was pretty much all outskirts.

It wasn't hard to find deer in Crestone. In fact, they were a nuisance; many of the yards had apple trees, and the town was inundated with deer attracted to them. Our first day, we hunted in mixed cottonwood and coniferous woods outside town but found no deer. The problem was, they were all in town, feasting on apples.

The second day, we arose at sunrise, had coffee, and headed out for another attempt. We got as far as the front porch. About 50 yards down the road that ran in front of the Bowers place was a loose herd of 30 or 40 deer, mostly does with a few bucks mixed in, standing there trying to decide which apple grove to invade.

Bob said, "Well, you're not going to get a better chance than this."

Using a porch pillar to steady my aim, I sighted on one of the bucks, fired, and missed. The deer all just stood there. "Your shot went high," said Bob, "aim lower."

So I aimed lower and dropped a buck in the middle of the road. This time, the rest of the deer got the message and scattered into the neighborhood. We dragged the dead buck off the road. While we were gutting him, an old woman pulled up in an old car and took pictures.

"You bastards!" she shrieked. "It's illegal to shoot deer on a road and to shoot inside the town limits! And these aren't wild deer, they're town deer. They're our pets. I know who you are and I'm going to report you!"

As soon as we got the gutted buck back to the Bowers place, another of the bucks who'd been in the road ran through the backyard and was jumping the surrounding 6-foot wooden fence when Bob fired off a snap shot and killed him in midair. Luckily, the animal fell back onto the Bowerses' side. Having shot all the deer we needed, we drove back to Alamosa that afternoon.

True to her threat, the old woman who'd accosted us reported us to the State game warden. A week later, he showed up at Bob's front door in East Alamosa with her photos and a signed complaint.

"I have a complaint of you and another guy shooting a deer on a road in Crestone, which wasn't legal," said the warden.

Bob studied the photos and said, "Without confirming or denying anything, I just want to point out that none of these photos shows a road. Where's the evidence that this deer was shot on a road?"

And it was true; we'd gutted the deer 30 feet off the road, and the woman, not being forensically trained by a long shot, had taken the photos from the road shoulder. In the photos, it looked like we were at the edge of nowhere rather than the edge of Crestone.

"Yeah, I know," said the warden. "Basically, it's your word against the complainant's. When I went up there to get her photos, I did look for the pile of guts, but the coyotes dragged them off."

Scratching his head, he continued, "I could still take it to court, but I don't think it'd hold up. If you do happen to be guilty, consider my visit as a warning. I'll also advise the old lady, next time she sees someone shooting a deer in Crestone—which I'm sure would never cross your mind—to get photos of the dead deer on the road."

Chapter 11 – Another wrestling room

She no longer thought in terms of the passage of days, weeks, months, years, but only of moments, cast seemingly at random across the calendar of the past, gathered together in her memory to provide revelations that would otherwise have passed unnoticed.

—From *Autumn Bridge* by Takashi Matsuoka

Eddie valued family and friends. He made one or two trips by bus each year to Los Angeles to visit his family. He also had a fairly steady stream of visitors to Alamosa. His old Army buddy, Louie, from St. Louis spent a week in Alamosa on two occasions, and Eddie reciprocated with at least one trip to St. Louis.

In the summers of 1965 and 1966, various siblings from Los Angeles visited. Lennie was the first, just after he graduated from high school in 1965. He held 1st- or 2nd-dan rank in kendo (Japanese swordsmanship) and brought his kendo uniform with him for a demonstration at the Armory dojo. In practice and competition, kendoists use a bamboo sword and wear protective head and body coverings. Lennie, however, performed an impressive kata with a full-length steel katana (sword), wearing only the black kendo gi and skirt-like trousers.

Kendo underwent a more severe decline than judo in the US during WWII, largely due to its association with swords, which Japanese were prohibited from owning By 1965, it'd recovered in the Los Angeles area, where around 250 people were practicing. Lean, mean, and handsome, Lennie was one of the top young competitors in southern California.

The next sibling to visit was Eddie's sister Carolyn (Keiko). A year older than I, she was what we called a "hot chick" in the odd vernacular of the 1960s. She brought along a light kimono and wore it to a teriyaki party at the Armory dojo. Her visit was touchy because most of us high-school guys developed crushes on her, yet we were careful not to look at her the wrong way with Eddie around. Maybe it wouldn't have been a problem, but no one wanted to find out.

The last to visit was Eddie's youngest brother, Stan, who everyone called "Squeaky." Twelve years old, he was a stereotypical, smiling, round-faced, short-haired Japanese kid inseparable from his baseball cap. He spent about 6 weeks with Eddie and practiced with us at the Armory dojo. With similar happy-go-lucky personalities, he and Eddie were kindred spirits. Around 40 years of age, Eddie was old enough to be his father.

Eddie's family in Alamosa was the judo club. In 1966 and 1967, at least four of us were juniors and then seniors in high school. With Rich Copenhagen living at Eddie's, we began occasionally stopping by Fridays after practice or hanging out there Saturday evenings. Eddie'd cook teriyaki and rice, and we'd talk, drink, and dance with Rich's girlfriend Connie and her friend Evelyn.

Suffice it to say, in addition to teaching us judo, Eddie taught us to drink. This wasn't dereliction on his part, for we were teenagers in small-town America—if we hadn't started drinking at his place, with someone to keep an eye on us, we'd surely have done it somewhere else.

I didn't much like alcohol then; three beers put me to sleep and any whiskey at all made me puke. I only got stumbling drunk once. I'd borrowed my father's car to drive to Eddie's, and when I drove home, Eddie laid out a return route that kept me on unpaved back roads, and he and Rich followed in Eddie's pickup. Okay, it didn't make much sense for two drunks to follow another one home, but I did go slow so I wouldn't lose them.

When I got home, I knocked over a lamp trying to navigate the dark living room. I thought I'd take some flak the next day, but all my mother said was, "Eddie called to tell me he followed you home last night to make sure you were okay."

That was it: no rebukes, not another word from my parents about underage drinking. Much later, I learned my father'd "been there, done that."

～

In 1966, possibly because the Vietnam War was heating up, the Colorado National Guard decided it once again needed the whole Armory building and asked SLV Judo to leave. I don't remember being involved in decommissioning the dojo—hauling out the frame, sawdust, and canvas—so maybe it occurred during the summer, when Larry Schnider and I were in Denver.

The next place we called a dojo was the wrestling room in the gymnasium at Adams State. We'd come full circle to another wrestling room after the high school 4 years previously. The room was fairly large, 30 or 40 feet square. The floor was entirely covered with a blue, plastic-foam, "insulite" mat, which was state of the art for school wrestling programs. Little more than an inch thick, it provided a markedly harder falling surface that we were accustomed to, and breakfalls tended to numb the hands. In addition, it was a slow surface, the rubbery texture impeding fast footwork. On the positive side, it gave fewer burns than our canvas mat and was level—we didn't need to dodge tire depressions.

Adjacent to the wrestling room was a gymnasium that had a 25-foot, 2-inch-diameter climbing rope hanging from the high ceiling. We never did weight training but relied on sit ups, standard pushups, judo pushups, and other exercises at the onset of each practice to build strength. The climbing rope was a good addition for strengthening arms and shoulders. At the outset, I could climb it only by using my arms and legs; after half a year, I could climb it up and down twice nonstop using only my arms, with my legs held horizontally.

The College gym also had large men's and women's locker rooms and adjacent showers. It was our poshest dojo. Our workout schedule continued to be 7–10 PM, Monday through Friday, and curiously we saw few people other than us. Adams State had an active wrestling program, but the mat room was in use only in the afternoons and not year around. A custodian apparently cleaned it after wrestling practices, for it never smelled bad.

Kurt Cary, a guy in the same school year as I, started judo about the time we moved to Adams State, having arrived in Alamosa the previous year. Athletically inclined, he played football his two years at Alamosa High. Unusual in being one of the few high-school varsity football players to join the judo club, he was a nice guy with an unassuming personality.

Kurt had some training in boxing and began bringing his gloves to judo practices so he could work out on punching and speed bags in the gymnasium next door. I was curious, so Kurt began bringing an extra set of gloves and teaching me to box. When he thought I had enough of the basics to do some sparring, we donned head protectors and went at it. Almost immediately, he connected a solid right hook to my head, and I went down like a rock, not out cold but seeing stars.

Kurt helped me up, laughing but concerned. "Matt! You don't seem to be able to learn to duck! I don't think boxing is for you—you'd better stick to judo." That was the end of my boxing lessons.

∽

It was curious that SLV Judo got permission for extended and extensive use of a College facility. A selling point may've been the many college students now in the judo club. Furthermore, around that time, Alamosa was actively campaigning to become an official training site for US Olympic Teams prior to the upcoming 1968 Olympics in Mexico City. At 7600 feet, Alamosa was higher than Mexico City (7350 feet), and both the excellent College athletic facilities and the elevation argued for a training facility there.

In October 1965, Judge Myers joined a delegation from the Valley that traveled to Denver to petition the Governor of Colorado, John Love, to support and fund Alamosa as a training site. The delegation included Jack Cotton, who was athletic director at Adams State, and Frank Powell, the College's acclaimed wrestling coach. Alamosa did become an official Olympic training site, and SLV Judo's access to the wrestling facility may've amounted to a quid pro quo for the Judge's support. Judge Myers could guffaw, glad-hand, and backslap with the best of them, but he didn't always do it for free.

Coach Powell himself started judo around the time we moved to Adams State, possibly with the encouragement of Bob Anderson, one of his star wrestlers, who'd been in judo for 2 years. The coach placed 3rd in the unlimited division in a tournament at Otero Junior College in 1967.

∽

The practices at Adams State in 1966–67 were heavily geared toward training for men's competition. A full half of each practice was occupied with hard randori, both standing and on the mat. The average age of club members was higher than before, with more college students and fewer juniors. I believe that few, if any, women remained by this time, although Sara Lucero was enrolled at Adams State and continued to practice. The younger women more than the men tended to drift off into other interests and activities, perhaps because there were few women's competitions and it was hard for them to maintain interest.

Some juniors were still attending. Harry Sumida (who we called Mr. Sumida) showed up from Fort Garland two or three times a week with Randy and Harry Jr., then 10 and 11 years old. For part of each practice, Mr. Sumida had them do seemingly endless rounds of uchikomi. I remember Randy literally weeping with exhaustion as he practiced his specialty, hane-goshi (hip spring), but Mr. Sumida was merciless—the boys continued until he said they could stop. If Eddie'd been less easy going, he might've objected to Mr. Sumida's intrusion into his class, but he never indicated it bothered him.

Mr. Sumida pointed out a flaw in my own judo, which was that I often lost the sleeve grip on my opponent when I attempted to throw. He said my hands needed strengthening and recommended I buy and squeeze a rubber ball made for this purpose. All of us might've benefited from his coaching, for he had a sharp eye for defects.

Born in 1924 in La Junta, Colorado, Harry Hideo Sumida was a year older than Eddie. His family was not interned during WWII because they already lived inland. He registered for the draft in Blanca in June 1942 but didn't enlist until January 1945, when he joined the US Army at Jefferson Barracks, Missouri. Mr. Sumida seemed very prosperous as a farmer. He was a pilot, with his own airplane and a private runway, and sometimes flew his sons to tournaments in Denver.

Mr. Sumida struck me as a hard man. I respected him, but his personality seemed the antithesis of "warm and fuzzy." Once I rode to a tournament in Denver with the Sumida family. The two Sumida boys and I were in the back seat. To pass the time, we played the license-plate game, seeing how many different states' plates we could spot among the cars we encountered. After disagreement about whether we'd already seen a particular state, Harry Jr. told me his family had a special technique for memorization. He was about tell me the technique, but Mr. Sumida glared at him in the rearview mirror.

"Harry!" he said, "You remember, don't you? We talked about this. The memory technique is a family thing, and we never share it outside the family. I mean it, Harry."

It was an awkward moment. Harry Jr. was embarrassed by the rebuke, and I felt distinctly unwelcome.

⌇

My regimen in 1966–67 was geared almost entirely toward judo and study. I got up at 7 AM and had breakfast, and my father dropped me off at school on his way to work. Afternoons, I rode the school bus or got a ride with Kent Myers, arriving home around 4 PM. A few afternoons a week, I did a 2-mile run from State Street to Highway 285 and back. I had a sandwich and relaxed until 6:30, when I left for judo practice. Returning home around 10:30, I ate leftovers or fried some deer steaks and then did homework until 1 AM or so.

Since we high-school seniors now had driver's licenses, we could get to tournaments by ourselves. Kent Myers and I drove to one Denver shiai that season as the only contingent from SLV. Leaving Denver early Sunday evening, we got caught in a snowstorm on the way back. Kent called home from Walsenburg, and the Judge advised us to overnight there. We found a seedy motel that, unbeknown to us, performed a dual function as a whorehouse. We got little sleep listening to drunken laughter, doors slamming, and beds squeaking the whole night. When the Judge learned where we'd stayed, he thought it was hilarious and ribbed us for weeks afterward, like "I let you borrow my car, and look where you go!"

That season, Kent placed 1st in a key tournament and qualified to represent the Rocky Mountain Region at either the US National Championships in Las Vegas or the US High School Championships in California, whichever he chose. He chose the US Nationals and attended a weeklong training camp at the Denver School in the spring to prepare but did not place.

A photograph taken after the 2-day Denver Invitational in March shows Eddie flanked by Kent Myers and me, with Harry Jr. and Randy Sumida standing in front. [Illustration, p. 162] The Sumida brothers are each holding a 1st-place trophy, and Kent and I 2nd-place trophies. I don't know whether we were the only contestants from SLV, or simply the only ones who'd placed. Eddie looks very dapper in a black suit, his usual attire at tournaments because he often served as judge or referee.

⌇

In May 1967, SLV reached a milestone. On 15 May, the *La Junta Tribune–Democrat* headlined a front-page story with "San Luis Valley wins judo meet," noting in the first paragraph, "It was a great day for folks from the San Luis Valley Sunday when the boys from San Luis won their first victory over the Denver School of Judo in the second annual Otero Junior College Judo Tournament."

Okay, it was a small tournament with only five clubs attending—SLV, the Denver School (DSJ), the Air Force Academy, Otero Judo Club, and the Arkansas Valley Judo Club—and it was a narrow win, 70–69 in aggregate score for 1st, 2nd, or 3rd places in the senior division. But hey, a win is a win.

The reporter for the *Tribune-Democrat* was probably initially unaware of the several-year rivalry between SLV and DSJ, with no inkling this was the first time we'd beaten them. I'm sure Judge Myers—or someone from SLV—soon informed him of this fact.

The reporter took some of the luster out of SLV's win by calling DSJ's lack of an entry in the 185-lb class a "fatal error" and implying that this figured heavily in Denver's loss. Nonetheless, he went on to note that it "... should not detract from the San Luis Valley Judo Club. They displayed a true go-go spirit, matching the Denverites with four firsts and three seconds." **[Illustration, p. 163]**

There was some faint praise for Denver too: "True to their advance billing, the Denverites placed in every event they entered." Well, so did SLV, but we had the foresight to enter a contestant in the 185-lb class.

This was probably the last tournament SLV attended in force. Four of us at La Junta—Kent and Carl Myers, Larry Couture, and I—had attended SLV's first judo lesson under Sammy Tahara four and a half years previously, and it was fitting we were together when we finally beat Denver.

～

The last competition of my SLV Judo career was the Rank Championships in May 1967. As a result of this tournament, Tooru Takamatsu himself promoted me to shodan, and I became the second SLV judoka to reach this rank. Two other SLV players were promoted as well. An undated clipping from the *Valley Courier* in May 1967 reads as follows:

SLV Judo Club Members Advance

The San Luis Valley Judo Club continued in its winning ways this past weekend, as they journeyed to Denver for the Rocky Mountain Association A.A.U. Judo Rank Championships, and three of the members were promoted to a higher rank.

Bob Anderson was promoted to the Sankyu Class, the first rank of the Brown Belt, Richard Copenhagen went up to the Nikyu Class, the second rank of Brown Belt, and Matthew Dick entered into the Shodan Class, the well-known Black Belt.

In tournament action, Bob Anderson won the Yonkyu Class event, the top of the White Belt, Matthew Dick topped all contestants in the Ikkyu Class, the top of the Brown Belt, and Kent Myers took first in the Shodan Class.

The day after the Rank Championships, Eddie, Rich, and I returned to Alamosa in Eddie's pickup. Eddie and Rich intended to polish off couple six-packs of beer on the way home to celebrate Rich's and my promotions, so I was the designated driver. It was a flawless spring day, and we took the scenic, mountainous back route through Leadville that enters the Valley from the north, rather than the usual flatter, faster route east of the Rockies. As I was inexperienced in mountain driving, it was a toss-up which was safer, I driving sober or one of the others driving drunk. Eddie kept interrupting his conversation with interjections like, "Hey, man, you're too close to the shoulder—watch it, or you're going to kill us all!"

〜

Toward the end of the school year in 1967, there were various activities for graduating high-school seniors, one of which was Senior Sneak Day. On a particular Friday, which was supposed to be secret, all seniors "snuck" out of classes and attended a day of outdoor fun at a place appropriately named Fun Valley near South Fork 75 miles west of Alamosa. Fun Valley was billed as a place where one could engage in "roller skating, miniature golf, fishing, horseback riding, dancing, hiking, croquet, and just laying around enjoying the warm sun." The writer meant "lying around" in the sun, but I'm sure there was some laying going on as well.

Fun Valley was not so much fun for our fellow judoka Kurt Cary. The footballers got liquored up and a little too rowdy, and Kurt ended up being thrown off an embankment. He landed badly, ruptured his spleen, and was rushed by ambulance to a hospital, barely surviving and losing his spleen in the process.

Laurier Couture and I, who'd for four years assiduously avoided anything that smacked of organized school activities except for things like science and photography clubs, snuck out of Senior Sneak Day and instead drove to La Veta Pass, where we parked on the shoulder of Highway 160 and climbed Sheep Mountain. We'd passed the mountain numerous times on our way to judo tournaments, and it beckoned to us. It was May 23, but at 10,620 feet elevation (nearly 4000 feet lower than Mt. Blanca), the mountaintop was already clear of snow except for scattered drifts.

Only 4.5 miles off the road, the peak of Sheep Mountain was not a long hike. There was no trail, however, and it was a difficult climb up steep talus slopes from the base to the long ridge leading to the top. The view from the top was worth the climb—Mt. Blanca and the Crestone Needles to the west and northwest, deep blue in the distance and still capped with snow; the magnificent, twinned, snow-topped Spanish Peaks to the southeast, like the milk-white bosom of Mother Earth herself; and the endless Great Plains to the east, a sea of yellowish brown and grayish green.

It was astounding good fortune to be in such spectacular country on a warm spring day and even better to be young in it. Whereas the ascent was slow and took hours, the descent took little more than an hour. We ran down the mountain, taking great, leaping bounds down what seemed like endless slides of fine scree. There was no thought of turning an ankle; we were invincible.

This was a fitting farewell to the Valley we'd both soon be leaving. It wasn't actually in the Valley but close enough.

I graduated from high school in May and during the summer of 1967 attended a 6-week Outward Bound course in the San Juan Mountains. A month after that, I left for college at the University of Alaska, Fairbanks. Others graduated and left as well—Kent Myers to Johns Hopkins in Baltimore, Laurier Couture to Colorado State University in Fort Collins, Bill Peterson to Southern Colorado State College in Pueblo. We continued practices at Adams State when we were in town that summer, but we were all short-timers, ready to fly the coop.

～

I can't write for anyone else, but a trivial story illustrates what judo did for me. October 1966 was the 4-year anniversary of our first judo lessons in the old high school on Main Street. One day that fall, early in my last year of high school, two little pachucos cornered me in a hallway just before lunch. One of them said, "Hey, man, we don't like you. You want to step outside?"

Neither of them was any bigger than Eddie, and if I knew their names, I've forgotten. I should've just laughed and declined, but it felt like a Fate-ordained test, as though a Higher Power'd thought, "Huh, Matt Dick is about to finish high school—let's see whether he's still a chickenshit." So I let curiosity overtake better judgement and said, "Yeah, okay, let's go." I wonder whether I'd have chosen this course if they'd been two *big* pachucos, or even one big pachuco.

We went out the back entrance on the way to the shop complex, one guy on each side of me like guards walking a death-row inmate. I thought we'd head out into the chico brush, but about 20 steps outside the door, while we were still on the sidewalk, the guy on my right tried to blindside me with a head punch. It was slow because he was right handed and had to stop to pivot in order to hit me (What a loser—he was as bad at fighting as I was!).

Before I even thought about what was happening, my judo reflexes kicked in; I gripped fast and tried to throw him with tai-otoshi. I wasn't in position either, and rather than falling, the guy went stumbling away off balance, his arms windmilling, and landed in the gutter. It was more an aikido technique than a judo throw.

The fight didn't get any farther. As I was turning my attention to the second guy, the school custodian, who happened to be working outdoors, shouted, "Hey, you guys, no fighting! Knock it off and get back inside or you're going to the Principal."

We went back inside, and that was the end of it. My opponents weren't very tenacious.

This burlesque of a fight brought full circle my school days in Alamosa from my humiliation in 8th grade just before I started judo. Once I'd decided to go along with the little gangsters, my state of mind was more an elevated awareness than fear. This relative calm in the face of threat—this internal confidence—was the gift Eddie gave me through the medium of judo, for which I've been ever grateful.

Chapter 12 – The later years

The purposes of this Act are to—(1) acknowledge the fundamental injustice of the evacuation, relocation, and internment of United States citizens and permanent resident aliens of Japanese ancestry during World War II; (2) apologize on behalf of the people of the United States for the evacuation, relocation, and internment of such citizens and permanent resident aliens; . . . (4) make restitution to those individuals of Japanese ancestry who were interned.

—PUBLIC LAW 100-383, Civil Liberties Act of 1988

Eddie kept the SLV Judo Club going for roughly 10 years after I left the Valley in 1967, though details are sketchy on where it practiced for some of that time. Late in 1967 or early in 1968, it moved from the Adams State gym to a small, rented building next to the Goal Post tavern on the east side of Highway 285 headed south out of Alamosa, again utilizing a sawdust-and-canvas mat. Rich Copenhagen remembers practicing there in 1968. Before Rich graduated and left Alamosa in June that year, Eddie promoted him to 1st dan, making him the third black belt I can confirm as having emerged from SLV Judo.

A business major at Adams State, Rich Copenhagen minored in physical education. In 1968, he took a methods class as part of the PE curriculum whereby he received academic credit for planning and teaching a course called "Judo and Self-defense." In April that year, he and two of his white-belt students competed in the 7th Annual National Collegiate Judo Championships held in Fort Collins, Colorado. Rich's course lasted for two quarters and involved about 40 students, some of whom continued in the SLV Judo Club after the course ended.

Bill Peterson, who was attending college in Pueblo, arranged with Eddie to return briefly to Alamosa in summer 1968 for a successful examination for promotion to brown belt. The exam consisted of Bill engaging in randori with Harold Hock, who probably ranked 1st-kyu brown belt by then.

Around 1968, Eddie switched from year-around work at Adams State to seasonal work from spring through fall. One of his main jobs in winter'd been chipping ice on the sidewalks, which he'd hated. Having his winters free meant he could migrate to a warmer place, and he did, spending time with his family in Los Angeles during the coldest months.

The few tournament results I've been able to find show some SLV judoka still competing after 1967. Rich Copenhagen placed 2nd in the 205-lb division in the Rocky Mountain Open Championships in Denver in 1968, and Randy and Harry Jr. Sumida 1st in the 11- and 12-year-old divisions at the Denver School's 16th Annual Invitational Tournament in 1969.

How long the club stayed in the dojo near the Goal Post is unclear, but it may've been several years, as I vaguely remember visiting that location on one of the next two occasions I was in Alamosa, March 1970 or August 1971. The existence of the dojo suggests Judge Myers was still involved with logistics, because Eddie didn't do logistics.

It's unclear where SLV Judo practiced between the time it left the Goal Post dojo (sometime after 1970 or 1971) and late 1974, when I again gained firsthand knowledge. Jeff Myers, who remained with SLV during this interval, remembers practicing for "quite a while" in the "old junior high school" (formerly the high school on Main Street, where the club began in 1962). He also recalls taekwondo practices held right after judo practices there, because he participated in both.

From 1974 to 1976, I returned to the Valley for two periods that totaled about a year. During the interval December 1974 to April 1975, SLV practiced at the gymnasium in Centauri High School near La Jara, 15 miles south of Alamosa, with students ranging from juniors to adults and including a few women. The club by that time was low-key, no longer focused on competition.

I returned again in September 1975 and lived near Monte Vista for about 7 months. By then, Eddie was sharing a house in southwest Alamosa with a guy named Manuel Olguin. Raised in Alamosa, Manuel'd been 2 years behind me in high school, though I didn't know him then. After high school, he did military service in Vietnam and then returned to his hometown, where he joined the police force. By 1975, he'd become Chief of Detectives. He and a patrolman on the force named Lionel Ortega were practicing in La Jara early in 1975, when I first got to know them. About the same height as Eddie, Manuel'd beefed himself up through bodybuilding to become a little fire plug of a man.

Around this time, Eddie and Manuel hatched a project to start their own dojo as a permanent home for the SLV Judo Club. Eddie loaned Manuel his entire savings of several thousand dollars for the construction or renovation of a small building next to Manuel's house and the purchase of mats. I remember the Imada-Olguin dojo as a small space, but a photograph taken there, probably in the first 4 months of 1976, shows Eddie and 16 club members ranging in age from grade school to adult and including one woman, Stephanie Weller, standing in judo gi in front of the large wall hanging of the SLV Judo emblem. Nearly everyone has a colored belt. **[Illustration, p. 165]**

Eddie's youngest brother Squeaky stayed with him in Alamosa for a period in 1976; 22 years old, he'd morphed from a little kid with a baseball cap to a longhaired California swinger. When I left Alamosa in the spring of 1976, Squeaky and I drove together in a 24-hour, nonstop marathon to Los Angeles. He and Eddie were very close, and it was a hard blow when Squeaky got caught in a riptide in California 3 years later and drowned at age 25.

Eddie's involvement with Manuel Olguin ended badly. In October 1977, Manuel and Lionel were driving downtown in Manuel's Lincoln Continental and stopped to confront a guy who'd supposedly been banging Lionel's wife. During the ensuing, probably drunken altercation, someone threw a brick that went through the big front window of Golda's Gift Shop. This behavior did not look good for members of the police force, and to cover it up, Manuel and Lionel arrested a vagrant man from Trinidad for throwing the brick and other fabricated offences. The guy had nothing to do with the altercation but spent 38 days in jail before he was exonerated.

Through the efforts of a local reporter, it all came out. Manuel and Lionel were suspended from the police force in December 1977 for official misconduct. During his tenure as Chief of Detectives, Manuel seemed to have a Napoleon complex and used his official power with a heavy hand. Evicted from the force, he was left with a lot of tough, mean pachucos bearing a grudge as enemies. Perhaps for his own protection, he sold his house and moved to Denver, without repaying the money Eddie'd loaned him for the dojo. It'd been a gentlemen's agreement with no paperwork, and Eddie had no legal recourse. He was very bitter about it.

According to Eddie, he asked Manuel, "How can you treat your friends like this?" Manuel replied, "Friends are cheap—I can get more whenever I need them."

Though Manuel escaped to Denver, Eddie stayed in Alamosa and may've faced some belligerence through his association with Manuel. This might explain a strange incident that occurred after Manuel left.

As background, early in 1975, my grandfather in Las Cruces, NM had a serious illness and ended up in the hospital. Since I happened to be in Alamosa, I went to Las Cruces to spend time with him. My aunt, who'd traveled there from Denver to help out, found a .38 revolver in his nightstand and gave it to me, saying she didn't want it around. When I got back to Alamosa, I mentioned the revolver to Eddie, who said, "Hey, man, if you don't need it, why don't you give it to me?" So I did, and forgot about it.

Sometime after Manuel escaped to Denver and I was back in Alaska, my sister phoned me. "You really shouldn't have given Eddie that pistol," she said. "He took it down to Beef's one night, and after he got a few beers in him, pulled it out and started waving it around, shouting he was going to blow everyone's head off."

No one got shot, and Eddie didn't get arrested. The reason I bring up this incident is that it suggests he was taking some rough flak from the Manuel-Lionel affair but wasn't going to take it lying down. He was like a pufferfish inflating its body and exposing its spines, saying to the carnivores around, "Mess with me at your own peril!"

⌐

As far as I know, the sale of Manuel's house and the dojo in 1978 was the absolute end of the San Luis Valley Judo Club, although the end may have come in December 1977 when Manuel was suspended from the police force. Assuming that SLV Judo ended in December 1977, it lasted for somewhat over 15 years, with Eddie as instructor for all but the initial 7 months under Sammy Tahara. Eddie ran the club for roughly 14 and a half years.

After the Manuel debacle, Eddie rented an old adobe house a few blocks from his previous place on Main Street and lived there with a Doberman pincer Manuel'd left behind. **[Illustration, p. 166]** He continued seasonal work at Adams State, where he'd become an institution, as indicated by a cartoon that appeared in the campus newspaper *South Coloradoan* on

16 October 1981. The cartoon shows a housewifely woman kneeling and planting flowers in a bed next to a sign reading "Adams State." Standing some distance away is a college administrator speaking to a short, long-haired guy with "Adams State" on the back of his jacket. The administrator is saying to the longhaired guy, "No Eddie, you have not been replaced. That's Mrs. Fulkerson." **[Illustration, p. 167]**

To understand the cartoon, the viewer had to know that Mrs. Fulkerson was the college president's wife and did her own gardening around the home the College provided for the president and his family. The viewer also had to know who "Eddie" was. Eddie normally tended all the flower beds on campus, and Mrs. Fulkerson would've been infringing on his domain—which I'm sure was fine with him, since it reduced his workload.

Eddie continued with seasonal work at Adams State into the mid-1980s, when he went to work one day and was informed he'd been laid off. This was so sudden and unceremonious after his more than 20 years of service to the College, it caused much bad feeling—Eddie felt he'd been treated harshly and unfairly, and his friends in town concurred. He was around 60 at that point and decided to retire.

I visited Eddie infrequently in the 1980s. His adobe house was minimal, mostly one big room, with a small kitchen and bathroom at the back, opposite the front door. The pipes froze in winter, and he had no running water for months on end. He sipped beer most of the day, with excursions to raid the dumpsters of the nearby Safeway supermarket or check his mail at the post office downtown, visiting friends along the way. It was fairly appalling to see the Sensei who'd given so freely of his time to so many people in the Valley living, as my sister described him, "Like a homeless person with a home."

Manuel's betrayal, the loss of Squeaky, and finally the loss of his job were hard blows, but when I saw him, he appeared more upbeat, cheerful, and content than his situation seemed to warrant. At home, he had his martial-arts books and the SLV team trophies scattered around. On one wall was a poster-sized caricature of Richard Nixon and Spiro Agnew dressed as Hell's Angels and sitting on motorcycles, both of them smoking joints and looking buzzed (Eddie's politics always were on the Liberal side). He had his Doberman companion and a canine successor when the Doberman passed away. In spirit, he was the same Eddie I'd known at the peak of the SLV Judo Club, and I hope his simple life was what he chose rather than forced on him by circumstances.

My sister Kathy remained in close touch with Eddie through the 1980s. He stopped by her office on Fourth Street downtown nearly every day to talk. She invited him to dinner at least once a month, asking which of his favorites he wanted, spaghetti or steak. It became an established ritual that, when he arrived at her place and saw what was for dinner, he'd complain. If he'd specified steak and she'd cooked that, he'd say in a disappointed tone, "Oh—I thought you were going to make spaghetti." If she'd made spaghetti, it was, "Oh—I thought you were going to make steak." Sometimes he brought past-date rolls or pastry he'd fished out of the Safeway dumpster, and Kathy had to find a tactful way to refuse those, claiming she was on a diet, or whatever. They always had a good time, rehashing the SLV Judo days and catching up on local news. By this time, Eddie'd been in Alamosa roughly a quarter-century, much longer than anywhere else he lived.

In the late 1980s, Eddie's friends in Alamosa increasingly worried about his living situation, and in 1991 Alyce Fujii phoned his family in California and suggested they come get him. This mirrored concern at the other end; Eddie's sister Carolyn summarized her recollection with, "My Auntie Hara (my dad's sister) lived in Glendale. She was worried about Eddie and asked Ron [one of Eddie's brothers] and me to bring him to stay with her." **[Illustration, p. 168]**

Carolyn and Ron flew from Los Angeles to Albuquerque in October 1991 and rented a car for the drive north to collect Eddie. When they showed up on his doorstep (he no longer had a telephone), he was glad to see them but resented their intrusion into his affairs and stridently resisted leaving. Finally, though, he went. It was fortuitous he did, because a year or two later one whole adobe wall of his house collapsed after an unusually heavy snowstorm. If he'd been next to it, it would've killed him.

My sister Kathy related another story that circulated about Eddie's resistance to leaving Alamosa. In acknowledgment of the injustice done to Japanese in the US by their incarceration during WWII, President Ronald Reagan signed into law the Civil Liberties Act of 1988, which authorized a compensation of $20,000 to each surviving internee. Payments under the Act began late in 1990 and continued to 1993. Alyce Fujii helped Eddie submit the paperwork for the settlement, which he received.

The story Kathy heard was that Eddie'd buried his settlement money in the floor of an old shed behind his house but'd forgotten exactly where and was vehement against leaving until he found it. I don't give this story much credence. Eddie might've been a bit eccentric by that time, but he had all his marbles and wasn't an idiot. If he'd buried the money, he wouldn't have left without it. At the very least, he'd have asked Carolyn and Ron to help him find it, but he didn't mention it to them at all. An explanation is that someone asked what he was going to do with his settlement, and Eddie, thinking it was a nosy question, gave a frivolous answer like, "I buried it in my shed."

Eddie stayed in Glendale with Fusako Hara until she passed away two years later in 1993. According to Carolyn, "we then found him a place in Norwalk, where he would walk every day for miles and collect 'stuff.' Later, [his brother] Leonard found him a place in Stockton."

Eddie passed away in Stockton in 1999 at age 73 and was interred in Cherokee Memorial Park in Lodi, California, having come nearly full circle to his birthplace in Sacramento. Fittingly, he was buried as a warrior. The inscription on his headstone reads, "Edwin J Imada – US Army – World War II – Jun 1 1925 – May 3 1999."

⌒

When I was in the judo club, I viewed the internment camps as a touchy issue. Eddie never volunteered to talk about Camp Amache, and I didn't press for information because the topic embarrassed me.

Laurier Couture and I once drove with him to a tournament in Denver. Eddie phoned an old friend and asked him to put the three of us up for the night. Laurier and I sacked out on the floor in sleeping bags, and Eddie took the couch. The friend'd also been in an internment camp, and I was curious why the Japanese community offered us Anglos hospitality after what they'd been through at our hands. I finally gathered the courage to ask the friend about this.

"A lot of us believe," he said, "that if the situation had been reversed, we'd have done the same thing to you."

The end of WWII didn't eliminate anti-Asian racism in the US, far from it, but in the 1960s it was less overt than previously. Eddie was sensitive to it nonetheless. For example, once after school I was passing through the Adams State campus and tracked him down to shoot the bull. An Anglo guy walking by some distance away was staring at us. Eddie muttered under his breath, "What are *you* looking at, *muthah-FUCKAH*?"

"Gee, Sensei," I said, "he probably doesn't mean any harm. Maybe he's just curious."

"I've had enough 'curious' to last a lifetime. But what do I know? I'm just a little Japanese Jew."

I heard Eddie apply this phrase to himself more than once over the years. The obvious connotation was his having been thrown into a concentration camp. There must've been a touch of bitterness to it, or he wouldn't have said it, but it seemed more wry or self-deprecatory than bitter in tone.

⌐

Eddie's relationship to his roots was complicated. He was fluent in spoken Japanese—he'd learned it at his grandmother's knee and it was probably his first language—though I never heard him speak it other than for judo terminology. Once we went to a restaurant in Denver that two of his friends, a husband and wife team, owned or ran. Eddie and the woman carried on a half-hour conversation, she in Japanese and he in English. On the other hand, my sister related that, years later, she and Eddie sometimes met at the home of Ben and Alyce Fujii in Alamosa for dinner, and that after Eddie got a few beers in him, he'd loosen up and speak Japanese with the Fujiis and other of their guests.

In 1975, I met up with Eddie in Los Angles and stayed for a week at the home of his parents and siblings. His father, Tom—around 70 by that time—belonged to an amateur group that performed shigin, an ancient Japanese singing art used for chanting classical poetry. I listened to Tom rehearse one evening as he sat at the kitchen table and later remarked to Eddie that it'd be interesting to hear the group perform.

"What do you want to listen to that shit for?" he said. "It sounds like a bunch of cats getting mangled."

In lieu of shigin as a Japanese cultural experience, Eddie took me to a theater in Hollywood that was showing a samurai porn flick. He assured me it was a classic of its genre. It opened with a bushido warrior torturing a beautiful, naked maiden. She was trussed into a wide-mesh net suspended from the ceiling by a rope, with her legs up around her ears and her rear end pointing down. As the warrior lowered her with the rope, she screamed, "Don't!—Stop!—Don't!—Stop!" Finally she was impaled on his engorged samurai phallus, on which he then began to rotate her. After a while, "Don't!—Stop!" changed to a panting "Don't stop! Don't stop! Don't stop!" The torture was that, unless she told him what he wanted to know, he'd stop rotating her.

That's all I remember. Corny, yes, but I had to admit—call me what you will—it was more entertaining than shigin.

It wasn't that Eddie rejected Japanese culture so much as he picked and chose, retaining aspects that interested him such as anything to do with the martial arts, including sumo, kendo, karate, jujitsu, and aikido in addition to judo. He knew at least a little about all of them and had some training in karate. He could also cook fantastic teriyaki. Ultimately, though, his relationship to Japan was like that of my father, a grandson of German immigrants, to Germany. My father didn't run around in Lederhosen, singing Die Lorelei. In fact, he showed disdain for his cultural heritage by flunking college German two semesters in a row.

On one of Eddie's annual trips from Alamosa to Los Angeles to spend a few weeks with his family, an incident occurred that he told with such wry indignation you couldn't help but laugh. He traveled by Continental Trailways, and the route involved first riding 25 miles east to Fort Garland, transferring there to a southbound bus to Albuquerque, and thence to a westbound bus.

Many Mexican nationals migrated seasonally to the Valley for farm work, and the US Border Patrol (called "La Migra" in the more Hispanic parts of the West) sporadically set up checkpoints for illegal immigrants. As Eddie was boarding the southbound bus in Fort Garland, a Border Patrol agent saw him from behind, pulled him out of the line, and asked in Spanish for his passport.

"Can you believe it?" Eddie related. "La Migra stopped me because they thought I was Mexican—they wanted to see my passport! I told them, 'I don't need a passport; I'm not Mexican. I am Japonés! I am Japonés!'"

᠊᠊᠊᠊

Without Judge Myers, a judo club wouldn't have gotten started in Alamosa—at least not when it did—let alone continue for as long or have such success as it did. It's unclear, however, how he got the idea for a judo club. Had he nurtured the idea before Sammy Tahara fortuitously showed up in his courtroom, or did that event spark the idea in his mind?

It's also unclear *why* he started the club. The proximate answer may be simple. Kent and Carl Myers were two years apart and, before the club started, constantly at one another's throats. Rich Copenhagen heard from Eddie that the Judge started judo at least partly so he could have some peace and quiet—that is, provide an external outlet for his sons' mutual aggression. Carl independently confirmed this.

The ultimate answer may be more complicated. For many years, I believed Judge Myers'd been a "helicopter dad," hovering above his son

Kent and relentlessly driving him to excellence and achievement. I now realize how flawed this view was. I believe Kent drove himself relentlessly from a young age, and that the Judge sought ways to productively channel his son's ambition and dampen his growing sense of superiority, if not arrogance. What could be better for this purpose than judo, which teaches respect for those above and below?

The Judge was a wise man and may also've wanted to steer Kent (and later Carl and Jeff) away from football, which more often than not rewarded qualities antithetical to those of judo. In small, Western towns, football was King. Players achieved high social status at school, and coaches'd do almost anything to win, sometimes to their players' detriment.

I don't know to what extent this applied to Alamosa, but when my mother taught high-school algebra in Trinidad, she saw firsthand the machinations of football coaches. They tried to acquire star players from other towns by offering the players' fathers perks and better jobs if they'd move. Coaches put intense pressure on teachers to pass footballers who were failing academically and wouldn't meet the minimum requirements for engaging in sports. In a contradictory instance, they convinced a skilled player to intentionally flunk his freshman year so he could play an extra year of varsity ball.

A direct downside to football was that a proportion of high schoolers had their knees ruined by bad blocks and tackles. The prestige of playing football wasn't worth being semi-crippled for life.

It was an intriguing coincidence that Judge Myers started the judo club the year before Kent entered high school and had it going strong by the end of his son's freshman year. This was exactly the period when it become evident that Kent would excel in football.

For whatever reasons the Judge initially started and fostered the judo club, I believe that once it got going, he saw how good it was for all of us—how it brought together people of widely different ages and backgrounds from across the Valley and gave purpose to kids who might've otherwise ended up in his courtroom.

Whitford Myers died at age 60 on 21 December 1980. His obituary lists his legal and judicial achievements but omits any mention of the SLV Judo Club, which I think ranks among his most significant accomplishments.

〜

The last time I saw Kent was in August 1971, 4 years after we'd left Alamosa for college. He'd graduated earlier that summer from Colorado

State University in premed, I from the University of Alaska in biology. He'd soon be on his way to medical school in Salt Lake City, I to a job in Fairbanks. We met one evening at Eddie's, where a small party was underway.

I'd seen Kent four or five evenings a week for several years in high school and spent countless hours in randori with him. While we hadn't been extremely close, hadn't shared much beneath a superficial, day-to-day level, we'd been friends. On this occasion, however, it felt like we were distant acquaintances, almost strangers.

Kent was now into karate, and his best bud in Alamosa that summer was a former classmate and fellow karate enthusiast from CSU, who'd arrived at Eddie's on a big motorcycle. Kent and I were sitting around drinking, conspicuously not talking at all about the past 4 years, when another of his karate buddies showed up, raving about how someone from a rival crowd'd just insulted Kent's crowd.

Kent jumped up, bellowing, "*What*? He said *that*? He can't get away with it. Let's go fuck those guys up *bad*!" There was a bellowing chorus from the motorcycle guy and the new arrival, "Yeah, let's go fuck 'em up!" They ran out the door in a rage, at that moment seeming little more than ambulatory sacks of muscles soaked in testosterone.

I had no desire to go fuck anyone up, but foolishly started to tag along. As I headed out the door behind them, Eddie took me by the arm.

"You stay here, Matthew," he said, "You're not a fighter."

I was taken aback. What did he mean, exactly? I'm still not sure, but if being a fighter meant willfully engaging in fights, maybe even instigating and enjoying them, then he was right—I wasn't one.

This incident raised other questions. Kent was soon to enter medical school to become a professional healer and, ultimately, a pillar of some community. Why was he heading out the door to "fuck someone up," ignoring Sammy Tahara's admonition in our first judo lesson 9 years before that street fighting was demeaning? Why'd Eddie stop me, yet say nothing to Kent?

Eddie was wise. He kept me from stupidly getting involved where I didn't belong. Perhaps he realized Kent was beyond words and would have to learn humility the hard way—or maybe he just viewed fighting and non-fighting as alternative, equally valid life choices. In both Kent's and my cases, he seemed non-judgmental, adhering to a philosophy of "live and let live."

I don't know how many students Eddie had across his 14.5 years of teaching judo in the Valley, but certainly they numbered well into the hundreds, as there was a lot of turnover. Some people started but lost interest after a year or two; others started in high school or college but moved on when they graduated (Jeff Myers may hold the record for a student's longevity in the club, starting by age 6 and continuing through high school). In a ripple effect, those of Eddie's students who went on themselves to teach judo amplified the number of people he affected, directly or indirectly.

SLV Judo produced at least three black belts (Kent Myers, Rich Copenhagen, and I). Various people recall that Sara Lucero reached 1st dan, though I've been unable to confirm this. Training four or five evenings a week and competing in four or five tournaments a year, Kent, Rich and I required between 3.5 and 4.5 years to progress from beginner to 1st dan. After 1967, SLV generally engaged much less in competition than before, and promotions would've been correspondingly slower, while there was still a lot of turnover. It thus remains an open question how many, if any, other people reached 1st-dan rank at SLV.

I vaguely remember that Eddie reached the rank of sandan (3rd dan) at some point, but I was unable to confirm this. After reaching nidan (2nd dan) in 1964, he'd have been eligible for promotion no later than 1967, given the depth of his service to judo. If he didn't reach at least sandan, he should have.

⌇

This ends the story of Eddie Imada and the San Luis Valley Judo Club, or at least the best I could do with it. While writing about Eddie, I could picture him in flesh and blood—his physical compactness, his demeanor and mannerisms—along with images of particular incidents and sound bites of conversation. Putting these things into words was a challenge I never expected to try to face. I wish I'd asked him more questions when I had the chance.

Eddie was one of the most deceptively simple, inherently complex people I've known. He never talked deeply about himself, at least not to me. He was bitter about some things, sad or regretful about others, but across 25 years I never saw him overtly angry, never heard him speak unkindly to another person.

His personality was the antithesis of arrogance and aggression. He was self-effacing rather than arrogant; able and willing to defend himself but never the aggressor. He was unflappable, centered around a solid core of self-reliance. He didn't want, need, or accumulate many material possessions. When he left Alamosa after 28 years, I'd be surprised if he took more than a couple suitcases with him.

I might go so far as to say he had a Zen approach to life—though he'd probably have laughed at that.

"*What*? You're crazy! Unberievabul."

Gardening was Eddie's vocation, judo his mission, and drinking beer his hobby. He kept them in their proper places, engaging in his hobby only after he'd finished with his vocation and mission on a given day. His hobby wasn't extreme; I never saw him what I'd call drunk, but at most pleasantly "buzzed." He was fun to be around, buzzed or unbuzzed, because he paid attention to and enjoyed the people around him. He valued family and friends above all else.

Eddie was an ordinary man of integrity, kindness, and humor. He was also the man who, in 4 years, guided a motley crew of small-town kids and young adults to the pinnacle of Rocky Mountain judo, and that was extraordinary.

Afterward

Currently in the U.S.A., these Japanese judoka [competing in the US] *are not in their best condition, yet they awe and for the most, go through our competitors like water through a funnel.* [They] *are splendid contest men, full of color, fight, and are real crowd pleasers. They are master contest strategists with outstanding judo techniques, but here in Japan, none of them were on the first team.*

—Donn Draeger, *Official AAU Judo Handbook*, 1963

Among all Eddie's students over the years, the only people I'm aware of who continued with judo as a lifelong pursuit were Kent Myers and Rich Copenhagen. Kent pursued premed education in Baltimore and Fort Collins and attended medical school in Salt Lake City, all cities with strong, active judo clubs. He was a silver medalist in the Collegiate Nationals in 1970 and 1971, and according to his brother Carl competed at a high level into his 50s. Kent reached 6th-dan rank, the coveted red-and-white belt, at age 68, two years before he died of a sudden heart attack. **[Illustration, p. 169]**

After graduating from Adams State, Rich Copenhagen worked in sales in Wisconsin, Illinois, Texas, and Missouri and kept up with judo wherever he went, remaining active in both competition and teaching. He reached 7th dan at age 73 on 15 May 2018 (after 20 years at 6th dan) and was still competing in the masters' division at age 75. **[Illustration, p. 170]** In addition to judo, he trained in aikido, taekwondo, and jujitsu, reaching 1st dan in taekwondo and 5th dan in jujitsu. At the time of this writing he remains active, teaching judo in Washington, Missouri at 77.

The Harry Sumida family moved to Arizona in the late 1960s,

and in 1970, Harry Jr. and Randy (representing the Dick Smith judo club in Phoenix) attended the Junior Judo National Championships in San Francisco. Among 682 contestants, Harry Jr. placed 2nd in the 15 years-light division, and Randy 3rd in the 14 years-light division. Randy went on to compete for San Jose State, placing 3rd in two US National Championships (Phoenix, 1974; Los Angeles, 1975) and 2nd in the Pan American Championships in Maracaibo (1976).

Bob Anderson, who reached brown-belt rank in the SLV Judo Club, achieved international prominence as a wrestler and wrestling coach. He describes his career as, "I am a national champion in all three [wrestling] styles—Greco, freestyle, and SAMBO—and I coached teams for the Olympics, Pan American Games, and World Cup." In the late 1970s, he was briefly involved with Gracie-family wrestling and jujitsu in Brazil, and perhaps his exposure to judo at SLV had something to do with that.

᠊᠊ᢙ

I kept up with judo only sporadically over the years, and these episodes allowed me a broader perspective on my years at SLV Judo. They made me realize how exceptional a sensei Eddie'd been, unpretentious, giving his best in such a way that made his students want to give their best. We worked hard but had fun at it. I later encountered some clubs as good as SLV but none better.

Surprisingly, when I arrived at the University of Alaska Fairbanks in September 1967, I found a moderately active judo club that met in the University wrestling room a couple evenings a week. It was run by Ken Hobson, a black belt in his 60s, who left Fairbanks a month or two after I arrived. This was unfortunate, because he was an excellent instructor, knowledgeable in self-defense training as well as judo.

A brown belt named Fred Ogden and I continued the club for two years. Fred'd started judo in Kodiak, a small town on the Gulf of Alaska, where Navy personnel ran a club. He later became active in judo in Washington state, ran a dojo in Yelm, and (at the time of this writing) holds 5th-dan rank.

᠊᠊ᢙ

In the summer of 1968, when I was working at a remote field station in Alaska and judo was the farthest thing from my mind, I received a letter from Dickie Okimoto and Jack Oliver in Denver. They alleged that Takamatsu Sensei'd been involved in the embezzlement of funds from the Denver School, and in a bid to somehow overturn him as head of the school or head of the Rocky Mountain Yudanshakai requested proxy for my vote as a black-belt member of the Yudanshakai.

I'd talked a lot with Dickie during the summer of 1966 when I trained in Denver. A year older than I, he'd been heavily engaged in youth-leadership activities in high school. He often repeated the adage, "Don't complain about a problem unless you have a solution for fixing it," which stuck with me because it actually is good advice. But did the "problem" they were trying to solve really exist?

Eddie was close to Takamatsu Sensei and told Rich Copenhagen around that time that Takamatsu'd used his personal resources, including mortgaging his home and possibly even bankrupting himself, to keep the Denver School afloat. What Dickie and Jack thought was embezzlement may simply've been Takamatsu Sensei paying himself back money he'd loaned to the Denver School. In any case, the Denver School had treasurers and auditors to deal with such issues. An unsupported allegation coming from two college students against one of the most eminent judoka in the US was ludicrous, and I sent my vote proxy to Takamatsu Sensei instead.

Apparently these differences got resolved, for a news blurb in the *Fort Collins Coloradoan* on 9 July 1976 announced that Tooru Takamatsu would conduct a teaching clinic at the Rocky Mountain Judo Dojo in Fort Collins, along with the instructor at the dojo, Jack Oliver, 3rd dan.

The Denver School of Judo continued at 2020 Arapahoe Street until 1981, when the large dojo was destroyed by fire.

Going into my sophomore year (1968–69) at university, I got the idea to teach judo as an elective sport in the school curriculum, just as Rich Copenhagen'd done at Adams State. The University agreed, although they neither paid me (which was okay) nor allowed me college credit for physical education classes (which I could've used). I ran the course just as Eddie'd run SLV. The wrestling room where the class met was poorly heated; the mats were thin, hard insulite, and falling on them was like falling on ice.

In 1969, Fred Ogden, a guy named Gary Woody, and I conducted a judo tournament at the University in Fairbanks. Fort Wainwright and Eielson Air Force Base were nearby and had judo clubs that could participate. Gary handled most of the mechanics of the tournament, while Fred and I competed, along with some of the students from my PE class.

The same year, Fred, three other university students, and I drove to Anchorage for a tournament at Ron Hildebrand's Anchorage School of Judo. That was the most miserable judo trip I ever took. The drive was 13 hours one-way in the middle of winter, with the five of us and our luggage crammed into Steve Wiren's fastback Mustang.

In the final match of my division, I went against Ron Hildebrand, who was about 35 years old and sported a bushy, Alaska-style beard. As soon as we gripped, he began muttering things like "Hey, man, you're gripping my beard, watch it!" I suppose he thought this sort of badgering would unnerve me. While he was busy grumbling about his beard, I threw him with a fairly nice uchi-mata.

A summer job in 1969 took me for several weeks to the tiny town of Bethel, Alaska, where by chance I encountered Noah Jack, a Yupik Eskimo who'd been in my PE class. We were delighted to see one another. We stopped by the town automotive-maintenance shop, where two of his male cousins worked. Noah and his cousins were all from some smaller village on the Yukon-Kuskokwim Delta, and the cousins spoke only Yupik. Noah explained that I was his judo teacher, and we demonstrated osoto-gari (major outer reaping). The cousins thought this was great fun and proceeded to throw one another onto the concrete floor of the shop, laughing like crazy. Damn, those Yupiks were tough.

In 1970, I competed in the Alaska State Judo Championship at Eielson Air Force Base, conducted by a sensei named Graham. His star competitor was a heavyweight brown belt named Jonas Edwards. Jonas'd occasionally practiced with us in Fairbanks, and I knew he was physically very strong and technically dangerous. We both placed 1st in our divisions, and I met him in the match for the state championship.

Graham was referee and said, "Since this is a championship match, there will be no time limit. You will fight until one of you wins."

With this, I lost the match before it started. I might've been able to withstand Jonas in definite increments of time, but infinity completely unnerved me. After 4 or 5 minutes, he pinned me and became state champion. Next time I saw him, he'd been promoted to black belt, which was a relief.

In 1978–79, I attended practices in Tacoma, Washington, held in the wrestling room of an old school on Yakima Street. The participants included juniors and seniors, men and women. The sensei was a Japanese-American whose name I've forgotten, which is a good thing, because those were probably the worst judo sessions I ever attended. After bowing in, he retreated to a corner like a wounded dog and basically let the class run itself. Only rarely did he demonstrate a throw. The wrestling mats were filthy, and my mat burns developed festering *Staphylococcus* infections that eventually required a visit to a doctor and antibiotics.

At one practice, the sensei designated a soldier from Fort Lewis to lead the warm-up. The soldier must've been in Ranger training, for he proceeded to have the class do 150 pushups. This was silly, because the juniors in the class struggled to do 10. I'd never in my life done 150 pushups in one go, but not to be outdone, gave it a shot. Though I didn't succeed, I could hardly bend my arms the next day and had trouble at work.

The only reasons I can fathom for the sensei's being there at all were that he had two young sons in judo and wanted to provide them the opportunity to continue, and that he was accumulating time-in-rank running a dojo so he'd be eligible for promotion.

A few years later, I attended some practices in the gym at Western Washington University in Bellingham. The young Anglo sensei mentioned that he'd recently placed in the Pan American Games, so I looked forward to learning from him. Most of the participants were university students, and most of them beginners.

The sensei led the warm-up exercises himself, one of which consisted of everyone jogging around the mat in a big circle. At his cue, we were to shout "hup-hup," or something like that. I wasn't in a "hup-hup" mood and didn't do it. During one of the first few practices I attended, he called me out of the "hup-hup" circle and publicly rebuked me.

"You're not showing team spirit here," he said. "When I tell you to do something, I expect you to do it. Team spirit is part of your training."

I didn't go back after that. Respect has to be earned, not demanded.

In 1990–92, I was living in New Haven, Connecticut and attended judo practices held twice a week in the gymnasium at Yale University. Though the club used a University facility, it was basically a town club, open free of charge to anyone and including juniors and seniors, men and women.

The sensei, an Anglo black belt in his late 20s or early 30s whose name I've forgotten, was excellent. His practices were structured much as Eddie's had been, and I learned from him.

Occasionally, a 5th-dan Anglo ronin showed up at the Yale practices. The term "ronin" originally applied to samurai warriors in feudal Japan who wandered as mercenaries, offering their services to anyone who could afford them. Nowadays in the martial arts, the term applies to someone who goes from club to club, practicing wherever his whims take him.

At the end of one practice, the ronin drew me aside. He had a new twist on applying or escaping from a particular choke hold and was nearly wetting his pants with the enthusiasm of showing it to me. He asked me to apply the technique to him. Unfortunately, I'd forgotten which choke went with the name he gave me.

"Jesus Christ!" he said, "And you call yourself a black belt! You're a good example of the rank inflation going on nowadays."

His remarks stung, for he didn't know anything about me and didn't bother to find out. I'd been out of judo in any serious context for 20 years and had forgotten some things. He could've refreshed my memory but instead left the mat in a huff.

My last foray into judo was with the Hokkaido University ("Hokudai") Judo Club in Sapporo, Japan, in 2004–05, when I was 54–55 years old. The University has a modern martial-arts gymnasium for aikido, kendo, judo, sumo, and karate. The judo club practiced 3–6 PM, Monday through Friday, with 20 or more participants showing up on a given day, most of them black belts but some of them beginners. I was working full time at the University and could spring free only for a couple hours here and there.

The head sensei was Dr. Hideyuki Matsuura, a biochemistry professor in the Department of Agriculture and former student member of the club. With a busy schedule, he was present infrequently, but other former club members still living in Sapporo often attended as sensei. When we bowed in at the first practice I attended, I was placed at the head of the row of sensei facing the students. I protested that I was just a visitor and should be with the students, but Matsuura Sensei explained that I wasn't a student any longer, that the lineup was in strict accordance with age, and since I was the oldest one there, I was where I belonged. This explained why people kept asking my age.

The practices were heavily geared toward training for competition. For warm-up, there was a minimum of calisthenics; instead, Wednesday afternoons were set aside for weight training. Ukemi practice was not part of the warm-up. Formal instruction was minimal; the black-belt university students took time out from their training to teach beginners. Practices involved group uchikomi for throwing, mat-work randori, and general randori. The formal instruction that did take place mostly dealt with mat work—how to turn over an opponent in defensive posture in order to pin him, the fine points of pins, and how to escape from them.

A 6th dan was associated with the Hokudai club and attended sporadically. When I met him, he presented me with a card that introduced him as a member of the Japan Businessmen's Judo Association. Once when Matsuura Sensei was absent, he gathered the students around for a pep talk. He spoke in Japanese but appeared to be exhorting them to focus more on throwing techniques during randori and competition.

The students listened with an air of bored sullenness that bordered on rudeness, which was surprising. The only reason I could see for this was that since the 6th dan'd never been formally associated with Hokkaido University, he was tolerated due to his rank but regarded as an outsider.

After a month of practicing at the Hokudai club, during which I'd routinely done the crawling exercises used to train for mat work, both my elbows swelled with fluid to the size of peaches. I thought I'd contracted a bad disease. One day at work, when my boss asked politely how judo practices were going, I showed him the elbows.

"Huh." he said, "You have lunch every day at the cafeteria. What do you eat?" I told him I usually had ramen noodles.

"Do you drink the broth when you eat ramen?" he asked. I replied that of course I drank the broth; it was delicious, so why would I waste it?

"That's your problem," he said. "The broth has a huge amount of salt in it, which is why we Japanese don't drink it. We just eat the noodles." And it was true; I quit eating ramen and my elbows returned to normal.

The Hokudai guys regarded anyone on the mat as fair game and showed me no mercy. That was okay; I didn't want to be babied. Curiously, I was the only one the 6th dan asked to do randori. In his early 60s, he was 8 years or so older and maybe 20 pounds heavier than I. He was still physically as solid as granite, and there was no doubt he'd been a formidable competitor. He threw me often and I couldn't throw him. A move he used frequently was to suddenly yank down hard on my sleeve and lapel. This caused an involuntary response that put me off balance, providing an opening for him. It was incredibly effective, and I wished I'd known it 40 years before.

In randori with the 6th dan, I soon began to feel like a punching bag. One day, however, I tried his own move on him, yanking down on his sleeve and lapel and immediately executing a footsweep. I caught him off guard and he went down for what would've been a waza-ari. In a reaction that surprised me, he sprung up off the mat furiously angry. He grabbed my right sleeve and gave my arm such a jerk that, ironically, it relocated a shoulder that unbeknown to me had been mildly dislocated for 20 years. I doubled over from the pain. The 6th dan realized something was wrong and asked if I wanted to stop, and I said yes.

Later he came up and said, "I apologize that I got angry with you."

I don't know whether I'd violated the vague stricture against throwing an older person of much higher rank, maybe so, but he wasn't that much older than I, and in truth, I was as surprised as he that I'd managed to throw him. The 6th dan may've lost some face that day, both for being thrown by a low-ranked foreigner and more so for getting angry about it, and I never saw him again.

It was an unfortunate incident, for I greatly respected the 6th dan, and the judoka at Hokudai would've done well to heed his advice. In 2005, I attended the Hokkaido Collegiate Judo Team Weight Division Championships held at Seisa Dohto University in Kita Hiroshima near Sapporo to watch Hokudai's seven-man team compete. Hokkaido Island is the northernmost province in Japan and the largest by area, so this tournament was equivalent to a state or regional competition in the US.

A small, 4-year private university, Dohto'd covered the floor of its gymnasium with enough tatami to provide three regulation-sized competition areas. The Dohto team beat every team they met 7–0, mostly with ippon throws, and won the championship for the 4th year in a row. One of the Hokudai guys lost by default (hansoku make) when he tried to leverage a standing arm bar into a throw. He must've figured it was worth a try, since he was bound to lose anyway.

The 6th dan'd been right; the Hokudai guys weren't training effectively. Their practices involved relatively little standing randori and no full-effort shiai practice matches, which Eddie'd used so effectively in preparing us for competition. They spent the bulk of their training time on mat work, whereas in the tournament most of them got thrown before they could engage in it. They didn't do randori with the 6th dan, by which they'd have benefited immensely.

Watching the Dohto tournament put my SLV experience into perspective. I believe that in my prime in 1967–69, I could've beaten most of the university students in the Hokudai club. On the other hand, most of the Dohto judoka were stronger than I'd been, and Dohto was far from being one of the top collegiate teams in Japan. In 2007, Dohto won the Hokkaido Collegiate Team Championships for the 6th consecutive year, again defeating every other team they met 7–0. In the National Collegiate Team Championships that year, however, they didn't even place among the top 16!

I don't know what skill level I might've reached if I'd trained after high school with a top university judo club in the US, like San Jose State, but I realized there were some very tough judoka in Japan, the likes of whom I'd never encountered. The truth can be a real bitch.

Sources

The newspaper *Mountain-Plains A.J.A. News* published by the Japanese community in Denver from 1961 to 1964 covered judo news in the Rocky Mountain region and was crucial in reconstructing the chronology of events related to the SLV Judo Club. Alamosa High School yearbooks likewise helped with chronology. The *Rocky Mountain JIHO*, other small Colorado newspapers, and *Black Belt Magazine* provided useful tidbits. For information on the Imada family, public databases on the Internet contained an amazing amount of detail in the form of census data, passport applications, ships' travel manifests, WWII internment records, marriage records, etc. I could find no archives online for the newspaper *Valley Courier* published in Alamosa, nor due to the pandemic could I easily return to the US to access paper or microfilm archives. Whitford Myers contributed to the *Courier* the results of at least some of the tournaments in which SLV Judo participated from 1963 to 1967, but I kept only one clipping.

[Abbreviations: DSJ, Denver School of Judo; SLVJC, San Luis Valley Judo Club.]

Books and book chapters

AAU (1963) 1963 **Official AAU Judo Handbook**. Amateur Athletic Union of U.S., New York, 288 pp.

AAU (1966) **Official A.A.U. – J.B.B.F. Judo Handbook**. Amateur Athletic Union of USA, New York, 318 pp.

AAU (1968) **Official A.A.U. – U.S.J.F. Judo Handbook**. Amateur Athletic Union of USA, New York, 352 pp.

Draeger, Donn (1963) **American judo also ran poorly**. In: 1963 Official AAU Judo Handbook, Amateur Athletic Union of U.S., New York, pp. 100–118.

Fuchigami, Robert Y (2020) **Amache Remembered: An American Concentration Camp 1942-1945**. BookCrafters, Parker, Colorado, 137 pp.

Inokuma, Isao & Noboyuki Sato (1979) **Best Judo**. Kodansha International, Tokyo, 256 pp.

Kano, Jigoro (2013) **Kodokan Judo**. 1st US Edition, Kodansha USA, New York, 264 pp.

Koiwai, E.K. (1966) **Women in judo: a medical standpoint**. In: Official A.A.U. - J.B.B.F. Judo Handbook, Amateur Athletic Union of USA, New York, p. 284.

Porter, Phil (1963) **The 1962 National AAU Judo Championships**. In: 1963 Official AAU Judo Handbook, Amateur Athletic Union of U.S., New York, pp. 22–45.

Simmons, Virginia McConnell & David Fridtjof Halaas (1999) **The San Luis Valley: Land of the Six-armed Cross**. 2nd Edition, University Press of Colorado, Niwot, Colorado, 364 pp.

Takamatsu, Tooru (1963) **America's most beautiful judo club: the Denver School of Judo**. In: 1963 Official AAU Judo Handbook, Amateur Athletic Union of U.S., New York, pp. 178–184.

Watson, Brian N (2008) **Judo Memoirs of Jigoro Kano – Early History of Judo**. Trafford Publishing, Bloomington, Indiana, 218 pp.

Young, Jerry (1966) **Women's judo**. Section 16 In: Official A.A.U. - J.B.B.F. Judo Handbook, Amateur Athletic Union of USA, New York, pp. 281–285.

Newspaper and magazine articles

Alamosa Journal (20 Mar. 1914, p. 1) **Court decides Mexican school case against board**. [Decision by Judge Holbrook desegregating the schools in Alamosa.]

Black Belt Magazine (June 1970, pp. 26–28) **Friction fractures judo factions**. [About bitter break between JBBF/USJF and AFJA/USJA, governing judo organizations in US.]

Fort Collins Coloradoan (19 Oct. 1965, p. 1) **Love to invite Olympic team to San Luis**. [About delegation from San Luis Valley to petition Governor Love for support for Alamosa as Olympic Training Site.]

Fort Collins Coloradoan (28 Apr. 1967, p. 13) **Judo tourney slated Saturday in CSU gym**. [Notice of "Novice" tournament that included all kyu ranks; "Adams State College" rather than SLVJC is listed as participating.]

Granada Pioneer (14 Nov. 1942, p. 5) **Fifty boys take judo**. [Short article about judo classes at Granada Relocation Center (Camp Amache)].

La Junta Tribune–Democrat (15 May 1967, pp. 1, 8); p. 1, **San Luis Valley wins judo meet**. [Article about second annual Otero Junior College Judo Tournament on 14 May. Photos, p. 8: winners in senior and junior divisions, with corresponding lists by weight division; action photos of Tab Ungkahkorn vs Matthew Dick (SLV), Wes Sterner vs Frank Powell (SLV), Clay Peacock vs C. Gray (SLV).]

Mountain-Plains AJA News (Mar. 1961, p. 1) **Denver Judo School plans moving to 2020 Arapahoe St.**

Mountain-Plains AJA News (Mar. 1961, p. 4) **Judo tournament champions**. [Reports some results from 7th Annual Rocky Mtn. Judo Tournament.]

Mountain-Plains AJA News (Sep. 1961, p. 4) **School of Judo**. [Reports fundraising for renovation of new DSJ dojo, and that work is underway.]

Mountain-Plains AJA News (Feb. 1962, p. 1) **Denver judo school dedication ceremony 'open house' Mar. 11**.

Mountain-Plains AJA News (Feb. 1962, p. 3) **Denver School of Judo, Inc.** [Full-page spread announcing open house for new DSJ dojo at 2020 Arapahoe; photos of T. Takamatsu, G. Kuramoto, Dr. T. Ito, and front of DSJ. Lists of yudansha and officers.]

Mountain-Plains AJA News (Mar. 1962, p. 3) [**Nearly full-page spread on ribbon-cutting ceremony for new DSJ**; letter of dedication; participating clubs and partial results of 1962 Rocky Mtn. AAU Open Judo Tourney. **Photos**: ribbon cutting with dignitaries; founders Fred Okimoto, George Kuramoto, and Tooru Takamatsu; DSJ trophy case; DSJ bronze plaque.]

Mountain-Plains AJA News (Mar. 1962, p. 6) **Denver judoists win Brown Belt Tourney**. [Main results of Open AAU Brown Belt Tournament at Lowry Air Force Base.]

Mountain-Plains AJA News (Apr. 1962, p. 6) **Denver judoists in Natl. A.A.U. Meet**. [List of 5 DSJ judoka to participate in National meet.]

Mountain-Plains AJA News (Apr. 1962, p. 7) [**Photo of Dr. Yoshio Ito** refereeing match at DSJ Promotional Tournament for juniors; photo of Ed Mizunaga, winner in 90-lb division.]

Mountain-Plains AJA News (June 1962, p. 6) **Denver Judo School**. [Note about summer schedule of DSJ.]

Mountain-Plains AJA News (Nov. 1962, p. 6) **Denver Judo School**. [List of junior, intermediate, and senior six-man team; Tooru Takamatsu named 1962–63 Judo Chairman for Rocky Mtn. Association of AAU.]

Mountain-Plains AJA News (Dec. 1962, p. 8) **Denver Judo School**. [Tooru Takamatsu attended Fort Hood Invitational Judo Tournament in Texas as JBBF representative.]

Mountain-Plains AJA News (Jan. 1963, p. 8) **Many judo activities**. [Announcements of dignitaries and judoka visiting from Japan; commencement of women's/girls' classes; list of some upcoming tournaments; unlabeled photo showing winners in Age-Group Tournament at DSJ.]

Mountain-Plains AJA News (Feb. 1963, p. 1) **Denver Judo School 10th anniversary**. [Announcement of anniversary celebration and annual invitational tournament.]

Mountain-Plains AJA News (Feb. 1963, p. 6) **Denver School of Judo tourneys**. [Completion of three tournaments, announcement of two more. Photos: winners of Novice Tournament; Wayne Fushimi & Tooru Takamatsu; Dickie Okimoto competing.]

Mountain-Plains AJA News (Feb. 1963, p. 7) **Denver School of Judo, Inc.** [Full-page spread with results of Brown Belt Tournament and Rocky Mtn. AAU Open Judo Championships, with photos: women's and girls' class with Prof. M. Ichinoe, Dr. Y. Ito, and Roger Stevens; Ichinoe and Dr. Ito teaching two women.]

Mountain-Plains AJA News (Feb. 1963, p. 10) **Judo school's food benefit April 21**. [Announcement of fundraising event at DSJ.]

Mountain-Plains AJA News (Mar. 1963, p. 1) **Rocky Mtn Judo Tournament 10th anniversary, Mar 30–31**. [Announcement of tournament; photo of Tooru Takamatsu.] **School of Judo Food Bazaar on Sun., Apr. 21**. [Announcement of chow mein benefit dinner at DSJ.]

Mountain-Plains AJA News (Mar. 1963, p. 9) **10th anniversary celebration at Denver School of Judo Sat. and Sun., Mar. 30–31**. [Full-page spread about DSJ; some history of DSJ; poster announcing 10th invitational tournament. Photos: 3-year-old throwing someone, and next to trophy; dignitaries from Japan. **Junior AAU Judo Champions**. [Photo and list of winners of Junior AAU Judo Olympic Championships.]

Mountain-Plains AJA News (May 1963, p. 10) **Yudanshas of the Denver School of Judo, Inc.** [List of Board of Examiners and judoka promoted to 1st dan on May 10, 1963, with photo of examiners and promotees; Eddie Imada at far left kneeling in photo, promoted to 1st dan. See also Sep., p. 6.]

Mountain-Plains AJA News (June 1963, p. 1) **Summer judo clinic during end of July**. [Announcement of AFJA (Armed Forces Judo Assn.) clinic at DSJ.]

Mountain-Plains AJA News (June 1963, p. 8) **Armed Forces judo clinic July 29–Aug. 10**. [More about AFJA clinic at DSJ; list of clinic instructors and ranks; notice of Open AAU tournament following the clinic.]

Mountain-Plains AJA News (June 1963, p. 9) **Promotions in rank at school of judo**. [List of promotions ranging from 5th kyu to 1st dan awarded in May 1963.]

Mountain-Plains AJA News (Sep. 1963, p. 6) **Rocky Mountain Regional Judo Black Belt Association**. [List of dan promotions registered with Kodokan on 25 July 1963; includes Eddie Imada's promotion to 1st dan. See also May, p. 10.]

Mountain-Plains AJA News (Oct. 1963, p. 6) **Denver School of Judo, Inc.** [Announcement of DSJ tuition increases effective Oct. 1.]

Mountain-Plains AJA News (Nov. 1963, p. 6) **School of Judo**. [Announcement of DSJ women traveling to CSU, Fort Collins, for a judo clinic; list of instructors.]

Mountain-Plains AJA News (Dec. 1963, p. 9) **Denver School of Judo, Inc.** [List of winners of Olympic Development Tournament on 15 Dec. 1964. **Schedule of judo events** [Announcement of eight shiai at DSJ and one in Colorado Springs; DSJ picnic.] Photo of front of DSJ at 2020 Arapahoe; description of school.

Mountain-Plains AJA News (Jan. 1964, p. 9) **Judo tournament for novices, on Sun., Feb. 9th**. [Announcement of date change.] Photo: match from Judo Junior Olympics in January.

Mountain-Plains AJA News (Jan. 1964, p. 10) **Junior Olympic Judo Tournament**. [List of participating clubs; full list and group photo of winners. Three judoka from SLVJC placed. This may have been the second tournament in which SLVJC participated.]

Mountain-Plains AJA News (Jan. 1964, p. 11) **Denver School of Judo, Inc.** [DSJ receives tax-exempt status as school; mentions names of legal counsel and of DSJ officers who attended hearing.]

Mountain-Plains AJA News (Feb. 1964, p. 1) **Rocky Mtn judo meet, Mar. 7–8**. [Announcement of 11th Invitational Tournament.]

Mountain-Plains AJA News (Feb. 1964, p. 7) **Brown Belt Judo Tourney winners**. [List of participating clubs and winners; SLVJC participated but did not place.] Photo: Denver School of Judo members on their return from Ogden (Utah) Invitational Judo Tournament.

Mountain-Plains AJA News (Apr. 1964, p. 6) **Denver judoists sweep Rocky Mt. A.A.U. Open Judo Championships**. [Participating clubs and full list of winners. SLVJC participated but did not place.]

Mountain-Plains AJA News (Summer 1964, p. 6) **Chicago judoists invade Colorado**. [Chicago judoka practice at DSJ in preparation for Junior Olympic Tournament in Colorado Springs on 25 July.]

Mountain-Plains AJA News (Summer 1964, p. 10) [Photo: **Jeannie Hall throwing Jack Oliver**; DSJ women preparing for Nationals in Mason City, Iowa, 11–13 Sept.]

Mountain-Plains AJA News (Sep. 1964, p. 8) **Denver girls defeat San Luis Valley**. [Delegation from DSJ traveled to Alamosa to inaugurate new dojo in Armory building; activities. DSJ girls perform Nage No Kata. DSJ and SLVJC seven-woman teams compete. Eddie Imada promoted to 2nd dan. Photos: Two women performing Nage No Kata; three Denver sensei with Eddie Imada; women's teams with Eddie and Tooru Takamatsu. Photographs by Whitford Myers.]

Mountain-Plains AJA News (Sep. 1964, p. 9) **Denver School of Judo**. [Lists of kyu-rank promotions for 75 men and women at DSJ on 25 Sept.]

Mountain-Plains AJA News (Dec. 1964, p. 1) **Judo tournament Sun., Jan. 10, 1965**. [Announcement of Kick-Off Judo Tournament at DSJ.]

Mountain-Plains AJA News (Dec. 1964, p. 6) **Denver judoists win in Salt Lake**. [Report of DSJ winners at tournament in Salt Lake City, Utah. Photo: Dickie Okimoto with Grand Champion trophy.] **Takamatsu named Chairman of Nat'l Board of Examiners**. [Tooru Takamatsu becomes national chairman of JBBF Board for promotions to 1st dan and above.]

Rocky Mountain JIHO (27 Feb. 1963, p. 2) **Technique applied by Hiro Tsubokawa**. [Photo showing woman judoka throwing Dr. Y. Ito, with Prof. Masao Ichinoe looking on. Mention of new girls' class at DSJ.]

Rocky Mountain JIHO (8 Jan. 1964) **Valley judo group names new instructor**. [Notice of first practice session of "reorganized" San Luis Valley Judo Club; delegation from Denver for the event; notification that Edwin Imada sent from DSJ as instructor; around 50 students in SLVJC will practice four nights/week.]

Spartan Daily (6 Apr. 1976, p. 4) **Judo team wins 15th title**. [Randy Sumida, sophomore at San Jose State and member of judo team, placed 1st in 154-lb division at NCAA National Judo Championships in Indiana, thus qualifying for Pan American Games and Olympic tryouts. Photo of Randy as university sophomore.]

Glossary

AAU—Amateur Athletic Union; the governing body for amateur athletics in the US in the 1960s.

aikido—a non-competitive martial art developed from jujitsu around the same time as judo, focusing on non-injurious self-defense against one or more assailants.

ashi-waza—foot (leg) techniques, a class of standing throwing techniques.

baka—fool.

breakfall—the technique of slapping the mat with the hand as one falls, in order to reduce the impact of falling.

bushido—the honor code of samurai warriors in feudal Japan.

chui—a "serious" prohibited act or penalty for same.

dan—instructor rank in the martial arts, as in 1st dan (shodan, 1st degree black belt).

deashi-harai—a throwing technique, meaning "advanced-foot sweep."

dojo—building or room where a martial art is practiced.

gi—martial-arts uniform, as in judo gi, or judo uniform.

Go Kyo No Waza—Five Groups of Instruction; the basic set of 40 standing throws used in judo, consisting of five groups of eight throws each, with the successive groups comprising techniques of increasing difficulty.

hane-goshi—a throwing technique, meaning "hip spring."

hansoku—a violation of the rules.

hansoku-make—a major violation of the rules or penalty for such.

harai-goshi—a throwing technique, meaning "sweeping hip."

IJF—International Judo Federation, the organization governing judo worldwide; sets international rules, organizes qualifying tournaments, and interfaces with Olympic judo.

ippon—one point, the score necessary to win a judo match.

issei—first generation, people who were born in Japan and immigrated to the US.

JACL—Japanese American Citizens League, a powerful organization for defending Japanese-American civil liberties in the US.

Japonés—(Spanish) Japanese; a Japanese person.

JBBF—Judo Black Belt Federation, the official, Kodokan-approved governing body for judo in the US in the early 1960s.

judo—means "the gentle way;" a sport derived from jiujutsu, without the dangerous striking and locking techniques of the latter.

judoka—practitioner of judo; judoist; judo player.

jujitsu (= jujutsu)—means "the gentle art;" precursor to judo, containing dangerous striking and locking techniques in addition to throwing and pinning techniques.

kani-basami—a throwing technique, literally "crab pinch," usually translated as "scissors throw."

kata—a highly stylized mode of practice whereby the thrower performs a particular set of techniques with ideal form, usually on both the right and left sides.

kata-guruma—a throwing technique, meaning "shoulder wheel."

katana—Japanese long sword.

kawazu-gake—a throwing technique, meaning "one leg entanglement."

keikoku— a "grave" prohibited act or penalty for same.

kendo—Japanese swordsmanship.

kibei—Japanese born in the US who travel to Japan at a young age to receive an education and then return to the US.

kiotsukete—means "attention," used to call people to attention before bowing.

Kodokan—judo's founding dojo, started by Jigoro Kano in Tokyo in 1882; now the Kodokan Judo Institute, headquarters of worldwide judo.

140

koka—a score previously used in competitive judo, valued less than yuko and non-cumulative, but capable of deciding an otherwise even match.

koshi-waza—hip techniques, a class of standing throwing techniques.

kouchi-gari—a throwing technique, meaning "minor inner reaping."

kyu—student rank in the martial arts, as in 3rd kyu (sankyu, 3rd student rank).

Migra, La—immigration; colloquial Spanish term referring to (in the 1960s) the US Immigration and Naturalization Service, including its daughter agency the US Border Patrol.

mirin—a sweet rice wine used for cooking.

morote-gari—a throwing technique, meaning "two-handed reaping."

Nage No Kata—The Kata of Throwing Techniques (see also "kata").

nage-waza—throwing techniques.

NCAA—National Collegiate Athletic Association.

nidan—2nd dan; 2nd degree black belt.

nipponjin—Japanese person.

nisei—second generation, US-born children of issei and automatically American citizens.

obi—belt.

o-goshi—a throwing technique, meaning "major hip."

(o)miai—match-making; the process of arranging a marriage.

osaekomi-waza—pinning techniques; mat work.

osoto-gari—a throwing technique, meaning "major outer reaping."

ouchi-gari—a throwing technique, meaning "major inner reaping."

pachuco/a—(Spanish) Latino gang member; small-time hood; tough guy/gal.

PTSD—posttraumatic stress disorder.

randori—free practice, or sparring, in which opponents use any permissible techniques against one another.

rei—bow.

ronin—originally, samurai warriors in feudal Japan who wandered as mercenaries, offering their services for hire; in the martial arts, someone who roves from club to club, practicing wherever his whims take him.

sake—in Japan, alcoholic beverages in general; in the West, rice wine for drinking (called "nihon-shu" in Japan).

samurai—member of the hereditary warrior class in feudal Japan.

sandan—3rd dan, 3rd degree black belt.

sansei—third generation, US-born children of nisei.

seiza—kneeling position, with trunk erect, shins under thighs, one foot over the other in the rear, hands on thighs.

sensei—teacher.

seoi-nage—a throwing technique, meaning "shoulder throw."

seoi-otoshi—a throwing technique, meaning "shoulder drop," combining elements of seoi-nage and tai-otoshi.

shiai—fighting-style tournament or competition.

shido—a minor violation of the rules or penalty for such.

shigin—an ancient Japanese singing art used for chanting classical poetry.

shodan—1st dan, 1st degree black belt.

shonen—age category in competition, meaning intermediates, aged 13 to 16.

shuji—Japanese brush calligraphy.

sumo—Japanese wrestling, in which standing opponents grapple inside a circular ring; one wins by causing his opponent to touch the mat with any part of the body except the feet, or to step out of the ring.

sutemi-waza—sacrifice throws.

tachi-waza—standing throwing techniques.

tatami—traditionally, roughly 3-foot by 6-foot mats used to cover floors in homes and temples; in the martial arts today, similar mats consisting of a layered foam core covered with tatami-textured vinyl.

teriyaki—meat or fish fried or grilled after marination in a mixture of soy sauce and sweet sake.

te-waza—hand techniques, a class of standing throwing techniques.

tori—the person applying a technique.

tsurikomi-goshi—a throwing technique, meaning "lift-pull hip."

uchikomi—"driving in" or "fitting," a mode of practice in which the thrower repeatedly gets in position for a throw but does not complete it; used to develop speed and form.

uchi-mata—a throwing technique, meaning "inner thigh reaping."

uke—the faller; the person against whom a technique is being applied.

ukemi—falling; the breakfall techniques used to fall safely in judo.

uki-waza—a throwing technique, meaning "floating technique."

ura-nage—a throwing technique, meaning "back throw."

waza-ari—half-point.

yata-kagami—eight-sided mirror with deep mythological and religious significance in Japan as one of three items that passed from the Gods to the first Emperor.

yonen—age category in competition, meaning kids aged 12 and under.

yudanshakai—regional black-belt association.

yuko—a score previously used in competitive judo, having a value less than a half-point and non-cumulative, but capable of deciding an otherwise even match.

Illustrations

View of Mt. Blanca and the San Luis Valley taken from Highway 285 south of Alamosa, with railroad tracks in the foreground. Photograph by Matthew Dick, January, 2015.

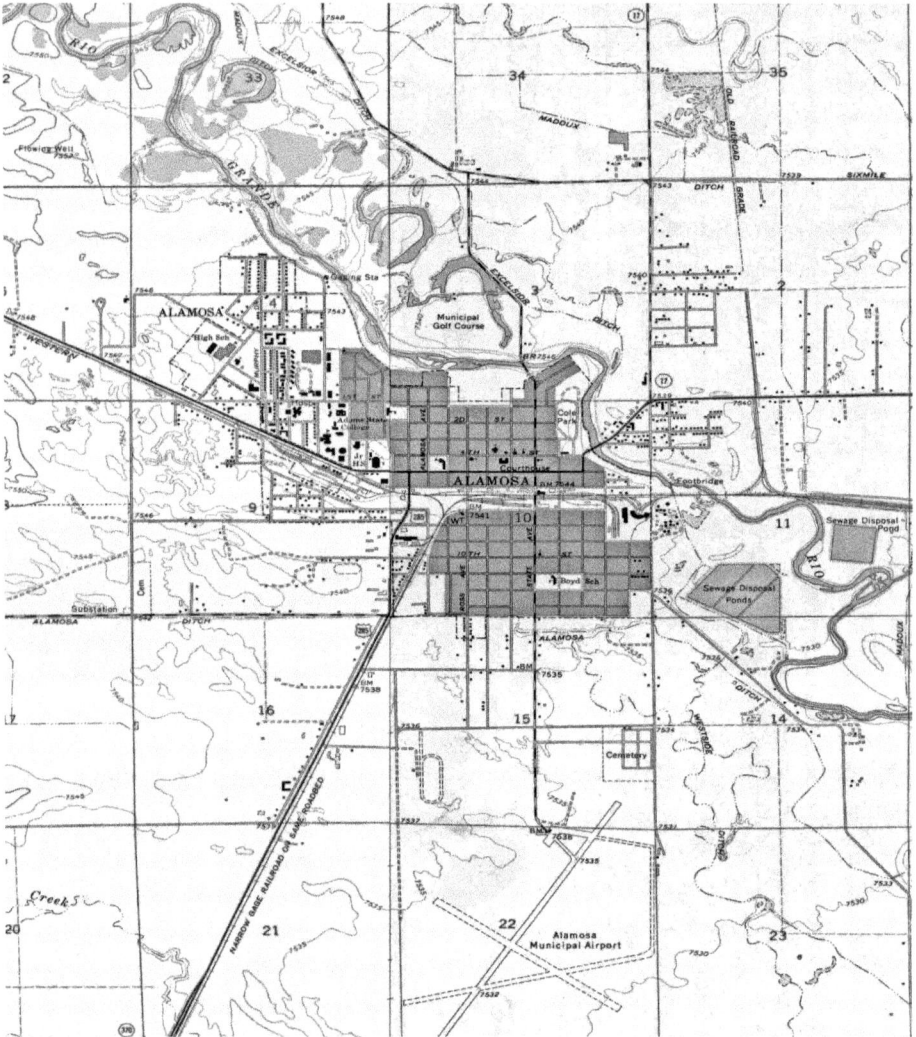

Topographic map showing Alamosa nestled along the southern bank of the Rio Grande River. Composite of Alamosa East 400019 and Alamosa West 400020, US Geological Survey, 1966; original scale 1:24,000.

Alamosa in the 1960s, looking west down Main Street at the intersection of Main and State.

Alamosa High School, first home of the San Luis Valley Judo Club, in 1963–64. View from across Main Street. Photo from *El Alarado* yearbook, 1964.

Judge Whitford W. Myers in 1965 at the time of his appointment to the Colorado 12th Judicial District, which includes the six counties of the San Luis Valley. From the *San Luis Valley Historian*, Vol. 9, No. 1, 1977.

Osamu "Sammy" Tahara at around age 80, Yokohama, Japan, 2015. Photograph by Matthew Dick.

Edwin Jun "Eddie" Imada at age 41, after the 14th Annual Invitational Tournament at the Denver School of Judo, March, 1967.

Tom Ichiji Imada (Eddie Imada's father) at age 19. Photograph from his US passport application in 1924.

Granada Relocation Center (Camp Amache) in southeastern Colorado, where the Imada family was interned during WWII. Photograph by Tom Parker, 20 June 1943. Denver Public Library, Western History Collection, X-6577.

152

New black belts and their examiners at the Denver School of Judo, 10 May 1963. Front row (kneeling), promoted to shodan (1st degree black belt): (L to R) **Eddie Imada**, Paul Okada, Ken Kuramoto, Steve Ishimoto, George Tagawa, Tom Tabuchi, Fred Yamashita, Ken Kinoshita. Standing, Board of Examiners: (L to R) Tooru Takamatusu, 6th dan; George Kuramoto, 4th dan; Fred Okimoto, 4th dan; James Sakabe, 2nd dan; Dr. Yoshio Ito, 2nd dan; Roger Stevens, 2nd dan; Jack Oliver, 1st dan; Leroy Abe, 1st dan; Stanley Zimmering, 1st dan. From the *Mountain-Plains AJA News*, May, 1963.

Rival insignia, San Luis Valley Judo Club (above) and
Denver School of Judo (below). The outer border and
center of the Denver patch are red, with the lettering
black. Photographs by Matthew Dick.

Laurier Couture's team windbreaker from the SLV Judo Club. Above, front side, with name sewn above the club insignia; below, reverse side with "ROCKY MTN." referring to the Rocky Mountain Yudanshakai. Photographs by Laurier Couture.

The Myers kids in judo gi at home in Alamosa ca. 1964; L to R, Jeff, Michele, Carl, and Kent. Photograph courtesy of the Myers family.

Eddie Imada with representatives from the Denver School of Judo at the inauguration of the Armory dojo in Alamosa on 22 August 1964. L to R, Tooru Takamatsu, 6th dan; James Sakabe, 3rd dan; Leroy Abe, 2nd dan; Eddie Imada, just promoted to 2nd dan. Photograph by Whitford Myers. From the *Mountain-Plains AJA News*, September 1964.

Certificate from the San Luis Valley Judo Club for Richard Copenhagen's promotion to yonkyu (4th kyu) on 14 July 1966, signed by Martha M. Dick (Secretary) and Robert J. Bowers (President). Courtesy of Rich Copenhagen.

Winners in the 12th Annual Invitational Tournament, Denver School of Judo, 13 and 14 March 1965, including three judoka from the San Luis Valley Judo Club: Harold Hock, standing 4th from right in front of the judo symbol; Harry Sumida, Jr., far left, middle row; Randy Sumida, far left, standing. Tooru Takamatsu, head instructor of the Denver School, is standing at the far right. Denver Buddhist Temple Judo archives.

The Denver School of Judo at 2020 Arapahoe Street. Above, interior view showing the trophy cases, stands, and mat area. Below, view of the exterior. Denver Buddhist Temple Judo archives.

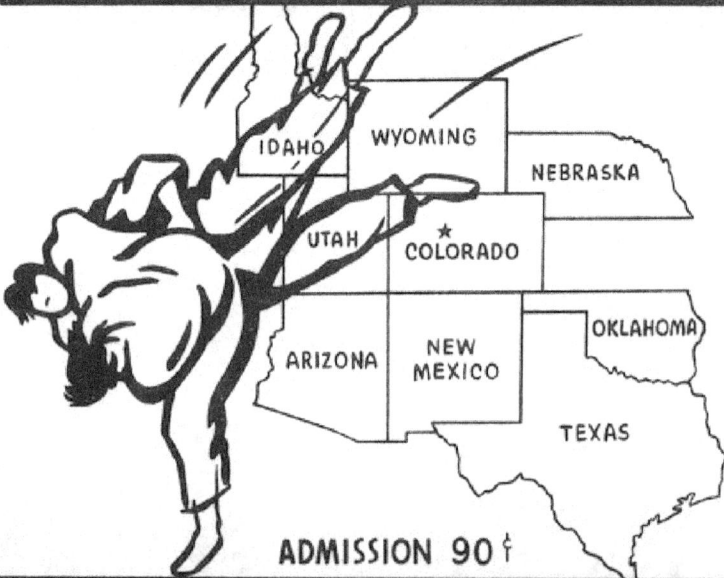

Advertisement for a judo tournament at the Denver School of Judo. From the *Mountain-Plains AJA News,* March, 1963.

Tooru Takamatsu, 6th dan. Above, photograph from the *Official AAU - JBBF Judo Handbook*, 1966. Below, refereeing a match at the Denver School of Judo (Denver Buddhist Temple Judo archives).

Winners from the San Luis Valley Judo Club after the 14th Annual Invitational Tournament, Denver School of Judo, March, 1967. L to R, Kent Myers, 2nd place; Harry Sumida, Jr., 1st place; coach Eddie Imada; Randy Sumida, 1st place; Matthew Dick, 2nd place.

Winners in the senior division, 2nd Annual Otero Junior College Judo Tournament, La Junta, Colorado, 14 May 1967. San Luis Valley Judo Club placed in every division and won the tournament. Judoka from SLV: Top row (1st place), 3rd from left, Matthew Dick, 155 lb; 4th from left, Kent Myers, 165 lb; 3rd from right, Bob Anderson, 185 lb; 2nd from right, Rich Copenhagen, 195 lb. Middle row (2nd place), far left, Laurier Couture, 135 lb; 2nd from left, Carl Myers, 145 lb; 4th from right, Everett Williams, 175 lb. Bottom row (3rd place), far right, Frank Powell, unlimited. From the *La Junta Tribune–Democrat*, 15 May 1967, p. 8.

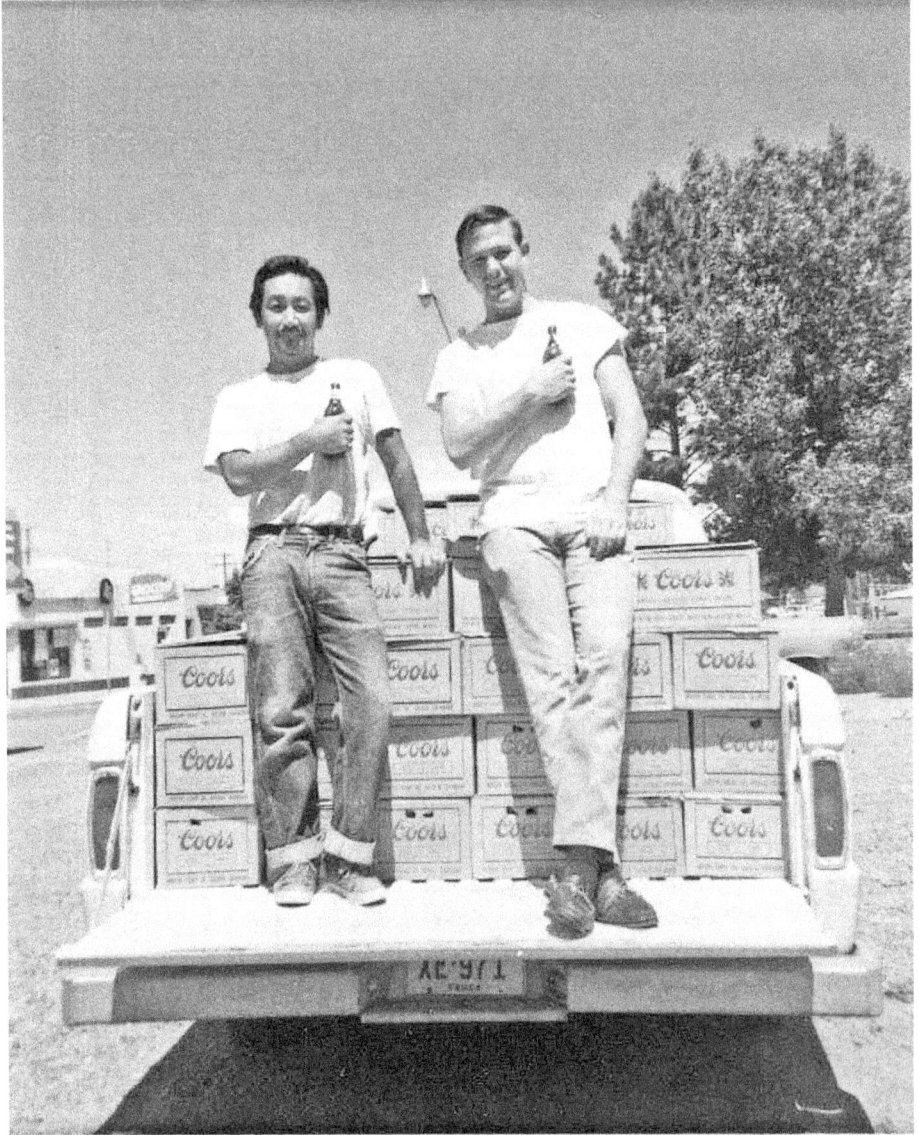

Eddie Imada and Rich Copenhagen standing on Eddie's pickup, ready to take part of their beer-bottle collection to recycling, around the time Rich graduated from Adams State in May 1968. Photograph courtesy of Rich Copenhagen.

The San Luis Valley Judo Club near the end of its life. The photograph was taken in the Imada-Olguin dojo, probably in 1976. Top row, L to R: Eddie Imada, unidentified, Jeff Myers, Stephanie Weller, Manuel Olguin, Dave Fukahara, Lionel Ortega, Matthew Dick. Middle row: unidentified except for Michael Olguin in center. Front row: unidentified except for Ernie Medina and Ricky Sloan, 2nd and 3rd from left.

Eddie Imada with his dog, in front of his house in Alamosa around 1982. Photograph by Matthew Dick.

Cartoon from the Adams State College newspaper *South Coloradoan* on 16 October 1981, showing that Eddie Imada was by that time a campus institution in his job as groundskeeper. Mrs. Fulkerson, the College President's wife, liked to tend her own flower beds around the President's campus housing, which was normally Eddie's job. Adams State College is now Adams State University.

Eddie Imada reminiscing with his aunt Fusako Hara in California, mid-1980s. Photograph courtesy of Carolyn Imada Lannon.

Kent Myers (left) after his promotion to rokudan (6th dan) at the Desert Judo Club in Glendale, Arizona, on 1 August 2018, standing with his son Ryan, who was promoted to shodan (1st dan) in the same ceremony. Photograph courtesy of the Myers family.

Rich Copenhagen and his wife Helen holding the certificate for Rich's promotion to shichidan (7th dan) on 15 May 2018. Rich is wearing his 1st-place medal from the 2018 USA Judo Senior National Championships. Photograph courtesy of Rich Copenhagen.

www.ingramcontent.com/pod-product-compliance
Lightning Source LLC
LaVergne TN
LVHW021447080426
835509LV00018B/2190